WOMEN [illegible]

A true 'WOMAN WARRIOR' LIFTS UP other women

BY KAREN MELONIE GOULD

Motivational Press
LEADERS IN GLOBAL PUBLISHING

Published by Motivational Press, Inc.
1777 Aurora Road
Melbourne, Florida, 32935
www.MotivationalPress.com

Manufactured in the United States of America.

ISBN: 978-1-62865-496-7

CONTENTS

INTRODUCTION

KAREN MELONIE GOULD

I AM THE FOUNDER/CEO of Gateway2Enterprise (G2E) the fastest-growing Alternative Finance Platform in the UK, one that has started and grown through finance, funding, finance business advice and a partnership with preferred suppliers.

We deliver Entrepreneur/Business Start-up/Growth Programs along with ILM Leadership and Management Programs from Level 2 to Level 7.

We work with organisations to sustain and grow their business through cultural change and development.

Having experience from working in many sectors from the international travel industry to the public and private sector, I have worked with some of the top FTSE companies in the UK.

Due to demand and our success, G2E has recently created its own team of Finance Finders to source the right kind of finance for the stage and culture of your business. G2E will make it pitch perfect and present this to funders, from crowdfunding platforms, venture capitalists, invoice financing to factoring and bridging loans. In 2015 we brokered successful agreements for finance from £1/2 million to £3.2 million in a range of ways from debt finance and crowdfunding to private equity.

I have my broker's licence to work in finance within the UK for personal wealth and have been approved by the Funding Circle as a Crowdfunding Broker.

I have mentored many businesses, from start-up to growth, in the last ten years and I myself have grown my own companies. My first business went from zero to a £10 million turnover within five years.

I have, through my mentoring skills, supported many sustainable and growth Small/Medium Enterprises (SME's) and many have won national and international awards.

G2E won the Runner-up Google Innovat8 Digital Award UK 2015 and were finalists for the Forward Ladies Best Start-up Business for Women 2015. In 2016, Gateway2Digital, a new offering from the Gateway2 brand, was a #VirginVOOM finalist.

I sit as a judge on the Midas Touch Panel in London, Fusion and MMU Manchester for Entrepreneurs/Dragons' Den. I am also a Venture Capital (VC) business angel.

I am a fellow of ILM and hold various training qualifications from CIPD, CMI, FETC, HETC and have an MBA in Business Administration. I am currently working on my Doctorate through publications in Switzerland.

I have also carried out numerous speaking engagements having been the international guest speaker in 2014, travelling to Berlin and Italy, speaking in 2015 in China and Prague with www.g-casa.com as well as at the Women's Leadership Conference in Milan, the Bristol Festival of Women Entrepreneurs and Business Show, Olympia, London. In 2016 I spoke in Singapore and Venice and delivered the Finance Pitching and Digital Pitching talk at the International Festival of Business in Liverpool, UK.

As an international author, with a publisher in New York, I have written several books, my last one being published in 2014 called *Happy Entrepreneur Mindset*.

Let me bring a colourful parachute of knowledge and expertise to develop and grow your business through the lens of finance.

W: www.gateway2enterprise.co.uk

M: +44 7939 164110

E: karen@gateway2enterprise.co.uk

Social Media: facebook.com/gateway2enterprise

uk.linkedin.com/in/karen-melonie-gould-g2e

@G2EUK |

UNIT 1

INTRODUCTION

KAREN MELONIE GOULD

ENTREPRENEUR FOUNDER OF UK FASTEST-GROWING FINTECH ORGANISATION

THROUGHOUT MY VARIED CAREER I have held many senior positions internationally, from being an Operations Director on the island of Jamaica for the biggest travel company in the world, to working in the public sector in the UK under Paul Boateng (an MP in London in the 90s), to working for the Department of Innovation and Skills with Pera at Grant Thornton with start-up loan contracts.

To working in academia as a mentor/consultant at UCLAN Preston, to lecturing at Salford University on their international MBA program, to supporting MBA students at MMU Manchester University via the Entrepreneur Program as a judge and mentor, to being a judge on their Dragon's Den, to actually coaching companies on the BBC 2 Dragon's Den programme, such as The Tea Company, who were successful to Klinked but did not feel this opportunity was for them and Oil Monster, who felt the same.

To working for private companies from Rockstar Mentoring Group as a consultant and business mentor, to working as a broker for Funding Circle and as National Sales Director for Business Scene (the biggest network organisation in the UK), to working as a consultant for local councils in the UK from MCC as Commissioning Manager in the Third Sector, to other London Authorities including Quangos from BGFF London, to NWDA NW.

In all my roles since I started my career, I have had the pleasure of being inspired and led by many a Woman Warrior. I came across my first influence when I worked for Harry Goodman, who owned Intasun in the 80s, with Joan Grimbaldson as my Resort Manager on the Costa del Sol in Spain. We had, as a team, the highest sales targets and customer service targets achievable throughout their programs. It soon became apparent to me why. Joan had the experience and the knowledge to lead and was thorough in her approach with our ground operations company and with hoteliers. We bonded immediately and became friends and in 1984 we achieved the highest sales targets in the organisation; my customer service approach led me to be featured in many national UK newspapers. Joan then asked me to stay on for the winter season and lead the team on running the golden program. Afterwards, Joan was headhunted by Airtours to go to the Caribbean and she took me with her as her Resort Manager in Jamaica. Joan today runs her own $1 billion travel company in Miami; because she mentored me, I went on to become the Operations Director in the USA and here I am today.

Then, whilst I was at Funway Vacations, my director of Customer Services was a woman named Pam, a lovely lady of Polish decent who sadly passed away some years later from the big C. Pam also mentored me in my role and the training I received there was so supportive, from leadership and management to PR—thank you.

Then when I returned to the UK, I was a consultant at BGCC, a London quango at the time, where I headed up Graduate Careers Training, Start-Ups and Business Development. I had a CEO who led with balls—and yes, she had a strap on as she took no prisoners. Jane M then went through a divorce and because she had two small children, she took the lead and instituted a nursery at work—not a move I endorsed then nor now, as I found female staff absent, checking on their children. The same thing happened when I was at MCC.

Jane also had a policy that on Friday mornings all staff, no matter if you had the school run, had to be in for 7:30 a.m. board meeting to present your reports and discuss your outputs and any issues. If you excelled, you then left at 12:00 p.m.; if not, you stayed until your work was completed.

For me, it was pure heaven. I was responsible for new contracts with City FTSE Companies, so tied those up and then would be out to take my new clients out for lunch and so on. I did respond well to this type of Woman Warrior. For other rewards, Jane introduced weekend bonding team trips away and Ireland was one I will never forget.

You could say that Jane introduced new and ground-breaking ways of working smarter, but they came out of finding a solution for her own needs – i.e. a single mum left with two small children.

Then I set up my two businesses, training and business support in London and dating in Brighton. I met in Brighton a beautiful, mature lady who had had a great career in banking before her marriage fell apart and her children left to go off to work and University. She started working for me part-time as an interviewer and host at my events. Katie was ideal for these roles, as she is beautiful, intelligent and extremely well-read, well-travelled and well dressed, with impeccable manners.

At the time, I was having problems in my own relationship and she coached me through one of the most difficult periods of my life. I was also drinking too much and abusing myself with being in a co-dependent and destructive, ruining my businesses and my life.

Katie was a true Woman Warrior: She had the corporate career and the great family life and then left it all to set up on her own in Brighton, as she wanted the freedom to live her life—she is still doing that.

Then I moved to the north-west of the UK and decided never to have my own business again; so went to work for a charity, the YMCA in Warrington, to use my finance and business development skills to secure them funds. This organisation was and still is run by their CEO Sue Blyth, who won an MBE for her services to the community. Though I greatly admired her and she meant well, I left after securing them over £750,000 in funds, as my vision for this organisation was to use the money for education and training, particularly for young girls and women to empower them to have the skills to become independent. I soon realised that Sue did not want this, as it took away her power and she enjoyed them staying "broken," unable to fly the nest or leave her centre. I noticed within the organisation that there were three generations in one family—mainly female—who relied on her centre, which to me was unhealthy and not holistic. I knew it was time for me to leave. Yes, Sue was a Woman Warrior, but she was frightened of change and could not accept it.

I moved on to MCC in commissioning for the third sector as a consultant in Children and Youth Services and Sue Douglas was the leader of these programmes. I had worked for Sue before in Education for MCC and I remember her words clearly to me the day of the interview: "Karen, I requested you for this role because of your skills in project management and finance, and I know you can get the job done on time and on budget—what I don't want from you, Karen, is any of your creativity." I did what it said on the tin under her leadership and managed twenty-six projects and a team of twenty on a budget of nearly £4 million, with a surplus to spend. Susan was a great leader on projects where I honed my skills. Susan took early retirement to follow her dream of running a B&B with her husband.

I then moved on to working in academia at UCLAN University and am still there part-time. In 2015 they won yet another business award for the Best Business Enabler Program within a University in the UK. I am a business mentor for them on various projects and in 2014/2015 focused on digital and creative projects. It was there in 2007 that I met Julia Stickley, who managed the programmes there and in the beginning, I mentored her daughter's first business—Danielle had a Youth Project in the early days. Julia and her daughter have to this day remained my friends and I have great admiration for Julia, as she manages to make a difference in so many people's lives.

I then went back to starting a business, this time in the third sector: a CIC community charity with CCO work, which I dissolved after a nine-year run during which we ran programs in the community targeting unemployment in deprived areas. This is my Work and Business Club and we probably helped over 500 people into employment, started over 250 new businesses and supported the growth of around 50 more. During this time I met some great women who are still my friends and colleagues still today, including Sheila, one of my closest friends who is in charge of the mentorship schedule in my programmes and advises me on HR issues. I will also never forget Emily – Kerry – Sharon – Christine – Anna – Anne and many more who have touched my life.

I then started another business, Workbiz Academy, a career management consultancy and wrote *Fast Track to Success* for Hope University Liverpool UK. During this period at Workbiz, I met and supported many women entrepreneurs who were mostly trying to juggle a family and a business around the kitchen table. I only dissolved this successful company in 2015 due to the growing demands of Gateway2enterprise, my current business.

During my time at Rockstar Group in the start-up programme, I, along with my team, probably helped over 2,000 businesses to start and grow. Though women have always been underrepresented in business programmes, I have met and supported some great women who are warriors in the 21st century, overcoming barriers of poverty, poor education, a lack of confidence and even the state of being single mums to start their businesses—thus creating independence, because having access to funds that they generate makes women great warriors!

Since launching Gateway2Enterprise in May 2014, I have been one of the few women in the UK until last month to be the CEO of a Fintech Company in Business Finance. Being that there are now over 113 in this arena, I believe you can still count them on your hands—including my partner Nicola Horlick from Money & Co., who was one of the first finance partners to join our platform and support us. We were runner-up in the Innovat8 Digital Awards UK, sponsored by Google, I and am in the finals of Forward Ladies UK Best Digital Business: Best Female Entrepreneur and Best Start-Up Business 2025, so we'll wait and see. It is the acknowledgement of and the participation with other women that makes it all worthwhile and fun.

ACKNOWLEDGEMENTS

Gratitude is a great blessing in life and I have been fortunate to have had the support of some great Women Warriors who are my friends and colleagues. Sadly, I can say that I don't have the support, nor the encouragement, of my family and they still to this day only try to discredit me and pull me down to their level. I have grown to live without them. There is not one female relative living who has inspired or motivated me or supported my journey and for that, I am relieved that I do not have to be in their company. I wish them peace and love and happiness, but my greatest wish is that they allow me to enjoy my life without them.

I wish to thank Sheila, Lucy, Christine, Ann and Kristen, who have remained supportive friends.

I also wish to thank some of my business partners and colleagues, who have become friends and have been supportive and encouraging, including Rav, Elizabeth, Jo, Carol, Nicola, Lizzie, Paolo, Penny and many more. These ladies are such an inspiration to me and this book is dedicated to all those Women Warriors whom I have met in my life to date: friends, colleagues, business partners, clients and more—this one is for you. Thank you sincerely for being Women Warriors.

In October 2015, I had the privilege to be the guest speaker at the World Festival of Female Entrepreneurs in Bristol, UK. I was the speaker on alternative finance with some of my colleagues (Nicola Horlick, etc.) and I want to take this opportunity to wish those inspirational women all the very best.

With thanks for your support of the Festival of Female Entrepreneurs. The event generated over 700 Women in Business.

On 23 October 2015, I was nominated by another amazing business woman for three awards: Best Digital, Best Growth and Best Start-Up for Forward Ladies Manchester UK. Though I did not win, I was amongst amazingly innovative businesses and in my eyes, we are all winners! My new Sales Manager and one of my new business mentors joined me—Angela Preston, an author and an inspirational and passionate lady.

ANGELA PRESTON:

I worked within the corporate world for twenty years in a leadership position, rising through the ranks to become a top performer within my field, before deciding last year to master my own destiny, to write a book and become a coach.

I am the author of *Opening Doors* and am also a motivational/inspirational speaker. The book is based on true life events of growing up in inner-city Liverpool in the 70s and 80s and I share my story of courage, ethics and success. My saying is, "There is a time for everything, but how does one recognise the time to leave or the time to open new doors?" I also do comedy events for charity and hosted a big event on the 20 November 2016 for Families Fighting for Justice, which is very dear to my heart.

My journey since writing my book has included being interviewed by both Radio City and Merseyside, as well as being featured in the *Liverpool Echo* as part of a story to do with the women's organisation. Authorhouse conducted a three-part interview with me on their Reader's Digest website, which was featured all over the world. I also completed a comedy course last year with the Liverpool Comedy Festival; again, the story of my performance was featured in the local paper.

My hobbies are really writing and travelling as much as I can. I am currently in the process of writing my second book, as well as writing a comedy play with my husband, which we are hoping will be aired on the radio. I am also busy being a mum to three wonderful boys, who have been my inspiration right throughout my life.

My life is so enriched to be surrounded by such talented and beautiful women. God, I am truly blessed. Thank you.

UNIT 2

INTRODUCTION TO OUR FIRST WOMEN WARRIOR

LADYWOMAN WARRIOR – LADY MURASAKI

MURASAKI **SHIKIBU,** OR **Lady Murasaki** as she is often known in English, was a Japanese novelist, poet and maid of honour of the imperial court during the Heian period of Japan.

"Murasaki Shikibu" Some scholars have postulated that her given name might have been **Fujiwara Takako**, recorded as the name of a lady-in-waiting ranked *shōji* on the 29th day of the first month, Kankō 4 (19 February 1007) although this theory has not been supported by many others. Her own diary, *The Murasaki Shikibu Diary,* states that she was nicknamed "Murasaki" ("Violet") at court, after a character in *The Tale of Genji*; "Shikibu" refers to her father's position in the Bureau of Ceremony.

My own inspiration for this book comes from my mother-in-law—yes, my mother-in-law, Kalifa, a true Bedouin Woman of Substance, rest in peace. I know you are looking over me every day with a smile and words of wisdom and encouragement. You were born before your time and struggled for the love of your family in a country and within a culture that is so cruel towards any woman—let alone a woman left to bring up her children and therefore become an unwitting entrepreneur just to put bread on the table.

UNIT 3

KALIFA: A BERBER WOMEN BORN BEFORE HER TIME

MY MOTHER-IN-LAW MEANING SUCCESSOR

As girls growing, we all dreamed of being a "woman of substance"—we all wanted to emulate her! I never imagined that my heroine would be a Berber woman of 87 years of age. Kalifa sadly died in 2007 and is who this book is dedicated to, as she inspired me in so many ways of which I was not aware at the time. Only after her death, when she comes to me in my dreams, do I understand the workings of her old wisdom. This is how the journey began …

Kalifa was born in Kairouan is a city in northern Tunisia's inland desert. It became a powerful trading hub and centre of Islamic scholarship in the 9th century when Aghlabid emirs ruled Kairouan and built many of its monuments. The Great Mosque, on the edge of the medina, with its antique columns and imposing minaret, dates from this period and is a major pilgrimage site. Born before her time in around 1920.

This was the dawning of emancipation, the birth of the "modern woman." Women were chaining themselves to railings for their right to vote; they were wearing shorter dresses with the short hair—all were signs of the coming of age of the modern woman! But Kalifa was born in the desert of Tunisia, born to Berber tribesmen, the nomads of the desert. The only certainty that Kalifa knew was that she would be, from birth, traded for land with a blood cousin to secure their bloodline and ensure the land would stay in their family.

She was born Kalifa Mhedhbii at thirteen she was as all Berber women were—dressed for the occasion in her traditional dress of red and gold, with as much gold as she could wear; her eyes were blackened by the dark kohl and her hennaed hands and feet paraded in front of my father-in-law, Amor Mhedhbi He was then nineteen years of age and a good match for Kalifa, as he was not a Berber but a young working-class lad from Benfica who already had a carpentry trade and whose father had olive groves.

The marriage bond was agreed to, even though Kalifa was no beauty by European standards. She was tall and willowy, with long, shiny, black hair that had a natural red sheen to it, which always glistened in the sun. She had a typical, angular Berber face, with a long Arab nose and slanted, almond black eyes with a full mouth, which my husband has inherited.

My husband, Fethi, is not just like her in her looks but still displays some of her mannerisms, as they were so close.

At seventeen Kalifa wed my father-in-law, Mr Amor, and went to live in a secluded village in Hammamet—two miles from the beautiful Bay of Hammamet, where I met my husband ten years ago.

Kalifa was taken from her home in the desert and given a home that consisted of a dwelling used to house animals like a cow shed. She lived there until she died and as her duty, bore Mr Amor thirteen sons and one daughter, from whom they have twenty-six grandchildren and seven great-grandchildren. Berber women, even though they are liberal compared to other Arabs, are there to bear sons, keep house and never question her husband and have no say in any issues in or outside of the home.

I believe Kalifa was that dutiful Berber wife and did fulfil her contract, though love was never mentioned or expected from her husband. According to old laws, Mr Amor could take another wife and did so when my husband was four. He moved to live with the other wife, though still returning to the family home weekly, where his wife was expected to satisfy his sexual needs. Another son was born, my brother-in-law Amed, who died tragically in 2005 in a car accident on his way home from college one sunny winter afternoon. I don't think Kalifa ever recovered from that loss. She had lost a daughter, who died swimming at the local beach and lost several of her children from the cold, the flu and other children's illnesses, in the western world, they would have survived.

Mr Amor is still alive though not well as he is well into his 90s' and did take again a much younger wife but since his health has become so poor she has decided to return to her family though as she is only in her 30s'.

Mr Amor has never had any time for his children, except one who was a gifted football player, who recently had an arranged marriage. He has always treated my husband with contempt and ignores anything he says; the only good thing he did do for us was to support our marriage, going against Kalifa to urge her to let go of her son to me to make a better life in England

When I first met Kalifa fifteen years ago, she greeted me on a hot, sunny May evening with false pleasure, which I saw in those glaring eyes. She weighed me up and thought, "This will be easy pickings for my son. She is a stupid tourist woman, older than my son, though she never knew exactly how much and would never believe it." Berber woman do not age well, with the childbearing, hard manual labour, starvation of love and affection and continual abuse from their husbands.

She greeted me in her new red and gold traditional dress and led me immediately to her son's room, where other members of the family had put together a bed, table—a "spider's web" to seduce and capture me for my money. I did not know it at that time, but they had a phone bill to pay and needed a bathroom and toilet built. She produced her ever-famous couscous with minimal tough meat. Of course, even though they are Muslims, the wine kept flowing.

Then Kalifa always led then in her "party piece" Berber music, where she would perform her barra barra dance with her new dance outfit, which she had changed into, made of silver, gold and lilac. She glowed in the attention, but more so from the adulation that she received from my husband. In years to come, I perfected this dance and would go on to perform this with her at weddings, etc. At first, it was not to her liking, as in the beginning, she was immensely jealous of me and the "true" affections from her son, whom she treasured above all and was "her love of her life"!

Kalifa brought up fourteen children single-handedly, with her husband often absent and no support from anyone. She was alone and often had to fend for herself and her children, even just to make ends meet and put a meal on the table. Berber women are not allowed to have control of any monies, to go shopping or pay bills—the men do all these duties. Though, when Mr Amor took another wife and Kalifa she had five small babies under five when it was freezing with no food in the house, what did she do?

My husband told me: "With all crying from the cold and hunger, she wrapped all five together in any blankets and clothes she could find, told them to keep each other warm, sung to them Berber folk songs, and told them to keep singing them until she returned." With their bellies rumbling and shivering together, Kalifa had to leave her small babies to find food.

She returned with the ingredients to make her own flatbread in her makeshift oven in the garden, where she taught me to make bread—a tin of harissa and a few herbs growing wild in the garden. My husband Fethi told me it was the best hot soup he had ever tasted and it filled their bellies and stopped them crying from the cold.

I had to live in the family house with Kalifa for six months during the winter and at times no one had any money, including myself. That woman could always be relied upon to rustle up a meal, put warmth in your belly and keep a fire burning from whatever she collected. No one ever went hungry or stayed cold and as for the love and support—the support was unconditional. She was the matriarch of the family, though only ever showed love to my husband. In the end, even though she wanted to hate me, she told my husband that I was better than any Berber daughter-in-law, that I cooked better and respected her! In the beginning, I used to fight with her daily, then we worked together in a partnership for the benefit of our family and for the love of my husband.

EPISODE – EID – MUSLIM CHRISTMAS DAY

It was Eid, nine years ago. I was living out my apprenticeship of six months to secure the marriage to my husband. My husband had been in an arranged marriage to Kalifa's sister's daughter—the best she could offer him. I came along and all her careful plans were destroyed—her son did the unforgivable and actually "fell in love" with me! She would not let him come to England, so she stood her ground, even against his father and said that if I really loved him, I would live in their house under their rules! In the beginning, I did continue to go and have lunch with friends, drink and come home late. But I was playing into her hands because that is what she wanted me to do. She knew I would do this, and then I was shown to her son what she thought I was: a shallow Western woman lacking all the qualities that she felt I did not display. I played her at her own game, in the beginning, to score points and irritate her—but I now I realise it was her respect I wanted, without knowing it!

I slowly learnt to cook Tunisian food, from baking flat bread in the traditional round oven in the garden to making couscous—but my biggest challenge came on Eid!

My husband and I awoke to a frosty, cold morning and torrential downpours! With no heating and no hot water, I knew I had to jump quickly from my bed with over a dozen horse blankets to dash from our room across the court, which was flooded, to our only toilet/shower with cold water.

It had to be done. Then, as I was about to count to 1-2-3 and "get this show on the road," Kalifa appeared—dressed—buzzing and rearing to go, with two cups of lukewarm, sugared chocolate. She told me that a bucket of hot water awaited me in the toilet room. With my improving Tunisian and her broken Tunisian, we always understood each other, with eye contact, body language and gestures and that empathy that we shared.

My husband was stirring, as he is so like his mother—always on the go, dashing around with lots of nervous energy. That is why they consume an enormous number of calories but remain tall and sleek. She wanted him to get ready quick and assist his father in cutting the sheep's throat and impress him that he was a man; she always wanted so much for Mr Amor to respect him. It never happened, unfortunately, in her lifetime and only upon her death did this happen—when my husband stood up to him over the handling of the funeral arrangements. They lived for each other and my husband's father put his mother in the ground while my husband was in transit, trying desperately to get home from Germany to bury his mother. He did not wait and that means closure is hard for my husband and he still cannot say goodbye!

I dashed across the courtyard with an old coat on my head and dived into the toilet room. I had a strip wash—oh, I was so grateful to Kalifa that morning for the hot, sugary chocolate and the hot water instead of frozen water on my skin, frightening anything that I might have picked up from the horse blankets.

We all gathered outside and watched my father-in-law and two older brothers perform their ritual. It did not phase me, as I was brought up on a farm in Kent—though our customs are slightly different! Kalifa was pushing my husband forward to impress my father-in-law, but the aggressive favourite son jumped in ahead of him and took away his big day. Kalifa's heart sank and I followed her eyes across the crowds—the tears like raindrops slowly formed down her cheeks as my husband was dismissed again.

Never mind, she would bounce back! The favourite son, Ziah, had a crate of beers to give to his father for the celebration after. We were skint. My husband had been trying to support Kalifa and me by working at the golf course as a caddie, collecting balls and giving lessons, anything, for £4 a day, something he had been doing since the age of four when his father left to support his mother.

By that time, I was assisting Kalifa and the other women in preparing the feast and she called me into her room and produced a rather dirty, crumpled twenty dinar note. She showed me under the bed that she had six bottles of rose wine, which she had been saving up. The plan was for me to hide the wine and when she gave the cue, present the wine from my husband to his father. Now, to hatch the other part of the plan, I was to make my way to the shop, across fields in a mudslide to purchase goodies for after the feast: tea, sugar, Coke, biscuits, yoghurt and tobacco for his father and sweets for the children. But how would I get there?

Kalifa presented me with a pair of her husband's socks and an old pair of his slippers. "Now off you go, quick!" I peered outside—the heavens had opened. I threw the old coat over my head and then hesitantly peered around the corner of the house to look at how dangerous the mudslides had become. Kalifa said to me, "I would do this, but I cannot leave the cooking on Eid—it is forbidden and Mr Amor would curse me, it is up to you." My husband then looked over from cutting up the sheep and said to his dad, "I will not let her go out there alone. It is my country and I know the route from being a young boy, I am going!" He threw down his knife and joined me by my side and said, "Come on, then!"

I followed him and just kept moving. He kept saying over and over again, "Come on, come on," and then finally, the shop was there. I pulled myself up the huge six stairs and nearly fell onto the counter. It was not a sight that anyone in Tesco's would welcome and indeed, I think I would be asked to leave! Like Hansel and Gretel, we eagerly ordered our treats. Then my husband said, "Now for the hard part, to get back uphill without losing the shopping! Just follow me and don't go anywhere else!"

Off we set, through at the first hurdle, I gradually slipped back down the hill and was covered in mud, with the red earth of the local terrain firmly stuck to my skin. My husband stood at the top and looked down. "Come on!" I cried, "Stop laughing at me. It is all right for you—it is your country and you know your way around even in the dark!" He came back for me and in the process slid down the hill; he grabbed that shopping as if his life depended on it! He picked me up, kissed me and said he loved me and said, "Come on, everyone is waiting for us—and we must not let down Kalifa."

As we turned to go into our family community, she was waiting there, anxious, trying to hide our absence from his father. The bucket of hot water was there again to clean me up. In the afternoon, we sat, my husband, myself, Kalifa and one of his nephews and laughed about our EID and shared our treats with the family and any neighbours that visited us that day.

SAF SAF - SCHOOL

Mr Amor had decided that no female would be educated in the family, as it was a waste of time and money to educate girls because we are not capable and only good for cooking, cleaning and carrying on the family line.

Whilst I was living there through a long, cold winter, I was bored. I did try to work and managed to secure a job in Sousse. I commuted on the train one hour each way, walking across the fields at 7 a.m. and having to take another pair of shoes, as I would be covered in mud. But, as Kalifa and my husband had said, it would not last. They both forbade me to go, but off I went. I lasted three days—the sexual intimidation was relentless and I gave up!

So, with time on my hands and being a teacher and facilitator of learning, I set about in the afternoons of holding school. It was difficult, because all the books I found were in French, as French is their preferred language at school there. Anyway, we had so much fun and I continued. Then the women wanted to join me and I had quite a full classroom, outside in the courtyard. Kalifa was against this in the beginning and sat across the courtyard staring me out and screwing up her face whilst peeling vegetables—because this is what girls should be doing.

So, I thought, if I combined cooking lessons with learning, then Kalifa could join in and take control—which is what I did. We all sat there wrapped up with our mint tea on bitter afternoons learning; and because I had won Kalifa, over Mr Amor never found out. And yes—two of my nieces go to school and one has gone onto beauty college to study. So, Kalifa was pioneering for a Berber woman to inspire education to female members of the family. She also continued to support me in the encouragement of education for the children and for the girls—this in itself was a true demonstration of her substance and how she was born ahead of her time.

Kalifa still comes to me in my dreams and she is still guiding me through life. She is surely a Woman of Substance, and I learnt much from the old Berber ways and incorporate these in my everyday modern ways as a woman. Her wisdom and her struggle will never leave me and has given me belief when I felt beaten.

There is a difference between being a woman entrepreneur and a Woman Warrior. I am going to allow you to make up your own mind of some of my examples. We all have the 'WOMEN WARRIOR' inside us but we need to unleash our power within.

UNIT 4

BUSINESS WOMEN WARRIORS IN THE UK TODAY

KARREN BRADY OBE – BOARD MEMBER OF BARCLAYS

"Not all women want to be prime minister... If they find balance, they're happy"

–Karren Brady

I WAS FORTUNATE ENOUGH to have worked with Karren Brady from *The Apprentice* in March 2014 in Chester. I caught up with her again when she presented a business event in Chester, UK in February 2015. Karren was the guest speaker at the Conservative Party event lunch in Chester, as she is an SME Ambassador for the Conservative Party and has recently won an OBE; she has become a board member for Barclays and has always been an inspiration to me. Karren was so supportive of my Rockstar Mentees, but also, in particular, Susan Kemp, from my Warrington Business Club and her Mums Entrepreneur Award in 2013 for baby massage. Karren also gave me some very practical advice, as I am about to launch another new business, as we entrepreneurs do. I noted what Karren said, but it is strange that it is the same advice that Richard Branson gave on his TV interview with Jonathan Ross on 2013: It is all about the PASSION: Is this what you wake up every day and jump out of bed to do? Always stay true to yourself, have foundations and maintain your integrity and keep a loyal team around you. It is advice I hold dear to my heart.

I reminded Karren at this event in 2015 of the advice she gave me and that I have valued this and taken that one thing with me—to "STAY TRUE TO YOURSELF," believe in yourself, to have the power to conquer all. Karen is, if that wasn't enough, closely involved with various high-profile companies—on the board of Philip Green's Taveta Investments and a management consultant to Simon Cowell's Syco. And now she's got a new title: Baroness Brady of Knightsbridge, sworn into the House of Lords as a Tory peer last November. Is it a nice finishing touch or the beginning of a new chapter—Karren Brady, political powerhouse?

Karren Brady began her career at Saatchi & Saatchi when she was eighteen years old and swiftly moved onto London Broadcasting Company as a sales executive. She joined Sport Newspapers Ltd. in 1988 and became a director within a year.

Karren is now known as the first woman in football. She was managing director of Birmingham City Football Club from 1993 to 2009 and during that time turned the Club's fortunes around. She took over Birmingham City FC when it was in administration and in her first year at the helm, the Club recorded a financial trading profit. In 1996 the Club made an overall profit for the first time in modern history and in February 1997, she launched the Club on the stock market; she was the youngest managing director of a PLC in the UK.

In October 2009, her business was valued at over £82 million and she sold it.

In January 2010, Karren was appointed Vice Chairman of West Ham United FC. In January 2011, under her leadership campaign, WHU was awarded as preferred bidder for the Olympic Stadium. Thus, her club West Ham United FC hope to be moving their post games in 2014. Following her first twelve months at West Ham, the club made a trading profit for the first time in many years.

Karren has attracted much media attention in her career and was the subject of an hour-long documentary, *Inside Story - The Real-Life Manageress*, shown on BBC1. She has hosted her own TV show and has also presented shows on it. Karren has written four books.

Karren is a columnist for *The Sun* newspaper, the UK's biggest-selling national daily newspaper. She is also a columnist for *Women & Home*. She is a judge of the Cosmopolitan Women of Achievement Awards, the Sports Industry Awards, Red Magazine Women Awards and Women & Home Women Awards.

An ambassador for The Stroke Association, Well Child and Teenage Cancer Trust, Karren is also chair of the Mothercare Group Foundation. She has been a board director of Mothercare PLC, Channel 4 Television and Sport England and is currently a non-executive director of Arcadia. She is an honoured fellow of the Institute of Sales and Marketing.

She was voted by *Cosmopolitan* as one of the 100 most powerful women in the world and in 2004 and again in 2006 attended the Queen's lunch for Women Achievers and Business Leaders. She was acknowledged as one of the most influential women in Britain by the *Daily Mail* and voted as one of Britain's Most Inspirational Women by *Good Housekeeping Magazine*.

In November 2006 she won the Cosmopolitan Woman of the Year, in the category of Women Who Have Changed the World.

In March 2006 she was chosen as the team leader on BBC1's *The Apprentice*, for Comic Relief, where she led her team (Trinny Woodall, Jo Brand, Cheryl Cole and Maureen Lipman) to a resounding victory over the boy's team (Alistair Campbell, Piers Morgan, Rupert Everett, Danny Baker and Ross Kemp), raising over £750k (the two teams together raising £1 million for charity).

In December 2007 Karren was a guest on Desert Island Discs and February 2008 saw the launch of Karren Brady's *'Today's Business Woman'* magazine.

In October 2007 Karren was voted Business Woman of the Year and in November 2008 she was named as one of the top leadership role models in a national poll. This recognition was quickly followed in December 2008 when she was presented with the coveted Spirit of Everywoman Award at the NatWest Everywoman Awards, acknowledging her outstanding achievements in changing the landscape for women in business.

During January 2009, Karren presented a series of features for iTV1's GMTV called *Just the Job*, helping people back into work and giving advice about looking for and retaining your job in this uncertain economic climate.

November 2010 saw Karren listed in the business category of *The Sunday Telegraph's* "100 Most Powerful Women in Britain," whilst she was also included in the *Evening Standard's* list of "London's 1,000 Most Influential People 2010," second to David Beckham in the category of Sport.

In December 2010 Dr Karren Brady received her Doctorate from the University of Birmingham in Business studies.

In 2010, following appearances as one of Lord Sugar's interrogators on the popular BBC show *The Apprentice*, Karren has replaced Margaret Mountford as Lord Sugar's right-hand woman.

In July 2011 she won the National Reality TV Award for Best TV Judge, beating Cheryl Cole, Louis Walsh and Alesha Dixon amongst others.

In February 2012, Karren was delighted to accept an appointment as an ambassador for the charitable organisation Wellbeing of Women.

Is this indeed not a Woman Warrior? I am looking forward to hearing more from Karren and her boardroom jokes, not so much boardroom but men's lock room – growing balls and walking around with a strap on etc. – as she said to us "WHO NEEDS to wear a skirt to attract attention and if you don't want to be Prime Minster being 'Happy' is a start."

WOMEN WARRIORS – NICOLA HORLICK

I have greatly admired this Woman Warrior since I worked in the City of London in the 80's 90's from afar. I never thought I would end up working with partnership in Alternative Finance and Investment with this special lady and to call a friend.

CAREER

Between 1982 and 1983, Horlick worked for her father in the family business. She then joined S. G. Warburg & Co. as a graduate trainee in 1983, starting in the investment management business, which later became Mercury Asset Management. She was appointed a director in 1989. She joined Morgan Grenfell Asset Management in 1991 and was appointed Managing Director of the UK investment business in 1992 until 1997. During the period that she managed that business, assets under management rose from £4 billion to £18 billion, she was ultimately suspended from the job on Jan 14 1997 and resigned two days later, after it was claimed she was moving to a rival and trying to get colleagues to join her.

She set up SG Asset Management in 1997 and Bramdean Asset Management LLP in 2004.[1] She was one of the founders of Rockpool Investments LLP in 2011 and was Chairman until 2015. She is currently the CEO of Money&Co., which is a person-to-business lending platform. She also has a film business called Derby Street Films.

PERSONAL PROFILE

Horlick has been described as *Superwoman* in the media for balancing her high-flying finance career with bringing up six children, Georgina, Alice, Serena, Antonia, Rupert, and Benjie. Her eldest daughter, Georgina, died of leukaemia in 1998 when she was 12 years old.

She married Tim Horlick, whom she met while at Oxford, in June 1984, when she was 23. They separated in December 2003 and divorced in 2005. Her second marriage is to Martin Baker, a writer and journalist, on 8 September 2006. They met in March 2005, when he interviewed her for the *Sunday Telegraph*..

SUCH AN HONOUR

I finally met Nicola on 29 May 4pm in the Little House in Mayfair to discuss Money&Co joining us through www.gateway2enterprise.co.uk as our Crowd Funding Platform. When I worked in London from 1989 – 1997, I greatly admired her but our paths never crossed even though I worked in the City of London. There is no doubt in my mind that she is a great lady both professionally and personally. Nicola is the original Superwoman but it is the way Nicola has overcome such personal tragedy, losing her daughter to leukaemia in 1998, that I admire most. The loss had an impact on one of her other daughters, Antonia, who was her youngest child at the time of losing Georgina and this family tragedy then saw Nicola having to struggle with another child, who was particularly affected by the long periods of separation from her mother whilst she was with Georgina in Great Ormond Street Hospital. Having gone through divorce and having lost a child myself, I can relate to her pain.

When I met Nicola I was so nervous as I had waited so long to meet her and she immediately made me feel comfortable and at ease and I felt her compassion and her genuine desire to support other women in business. I was overwhelmed as she told me about all her business ventures from film development to NHS Board Member . She told me about the restaurant that she had set up that had struggled, but she hadn't given up and had changed the business concept to a bar with food and moved it to another location. We ENTREPRENEUR WOMEN WARRIORS strive to survive professionally and personally and always will but to have another woman be supportive – tell me about it - it is not only refreshing but such an inspiration to me and to other women out there who are trying to 'not have it all' but take the responsibility of our own careers – money and support our family and friends. I am sure that Nicola and I will continue to work together in the future and be supportive of each other. Being an entrepreneur can be lonely at times, particularly when you are a woman as you wear so many other hats and sometimes other women are not always as supportive as we would like.

After I met Nicola, I facilitated events for Money&Co. in the North of England and this ALTERNATIVE FUNDING PLATFORM is now one of my partners.

Nicola supported me in 2016, when she was a keynote speaker at IFB2016 and a judge for my Pitching Battles and I know that as a genuine female entrepreneur I can always count on her support as she is a Woman Warrior

UNIT 5

MUMSNET ENTREPRENEURS

SUSAN KEMP - BABY MASSAGE ON MY BUSINESS CLUB 2012
WARRINGTON CHESHIRE UK

I MET SUSAN IN 2012 when she took the Business Enterprise Scheme in Warrington. Following a family move to the North West from London, Susan had to give up her job in communications in a major media publisher. Unable to find a job with flexibility, she decided to start her own business. She sought guidance with starting and running her own business whilst being able to draw upon skills she already had. Susan created a baby massage tuition business teaching new parents skills of massage and yoga, creating a community activity and a niche business. This allows her to control her own working hours and flexibility so she can be around for her young daughter. Susan has won awards for her business start-up and the business has thrived becoming a must-do activity amongst new parents within the local area.

Appleton Baby Massage

January 2014

Baby massage continues to grow and strengthens with baby yoga

I am the owner and instructor of Appleton Baby Massage, which offers baby massage and baby yoga classes for new mums, which teach them how to massage and perform yoga with their baby in a structured course.

The business is based in Appleton and serves mums from Warrington and the surrounding areas of Cheshire.

Since setting up business in December 2012, I have welcomed over 100 mums and babies. Appleton Baby Massage has now become a talked-about and "must-do" activity amongst new mums.

As a mum myself, I understand what new mums want and I'm proud that I offer more than just an activity; I provide small group classes in a homely environment with the added touch of tea and home-baked cakes to encourage chat. My business is continually growing and I've further developed with the addition of baby yoga classes, which is the perfect follow-on from baby massage.

I undertook the Workbiz Business Enterprise program in 2012 after I had given up my role as communications manager at the *Daily Mail* group following a family move to the North West. I needed a job to suit family life and therefore, I re-trained as a baby massage instructor.

The program gave me the confidence and business know-how to work for myself. The business advice received was invaluable, giving me the good, solid foundation I needed to start my business. I learnt from experts within the field of finance to help with cash flow management and from marketers to refresh and extend my marketing and social media knowledge.

I was able to reach out to them for additional guidance and support. I had a wonderful mentor who was incredibly supportive. I was given encouragement, ideas and direction through the new world of business. It was such boost and comfort to have an empathetic mentor I could turn to for guidance.

I was awarded Business Start-Up of the Year 2012 by the Workbiz Club. I felt empowered to utilise my marketing skills to create my own brand, develop a website and promotional material and promote myself with confidence. I am regularly invited to give talks to expectant parents at events and I've gained support from local antenatal and baby health professionals.

UNIT 6

MUMS, GRANDMOTHERS, ETC.

My great-grandmother, Mrs Chamberlin, was a strong woman though small in stature she was a Woman Warrior.

My memories of my great-grandmother were that she was very strict and old school, though I did not please her—she thought of me as insolent and too cheeky, which was probably true. She had thrombosis in her left leg and this had to be amputated.

She was small, of a slim build. During her later years, she came to live with my grandmother Isabella in the Kent countryside and spent her last years there, with my grandmother caring for her. I must admit I used to taunt her with stealing her money and digesting pennies; then my grandmother had to force cod liver oil down my throat to make me go to the toilet, so my grandmother could fish out the money from the toilet basin. She insisted on having it back—washed, of course.

I thought my great-grandmother did not like me, but during my time living with my grandmother on our return from Australia, she would come to me—not in my dreams, but in my grandmother's bedroom when I said her name and spoke to her. I used to sleep with my grandmother and my great-grandmother would tell me that I had a big journey ahead of me and that my grandmother needed me, but that I would make her and my grandmother proud—and I did.

I qualified as a teacher and became the youngest teacher in Kent, teaching in Further Education at that time. I would have made my grandmother more proud if I could have married my childhood sweetheart, Shaun. This I did not do, but we remain great friends to this day.

My grandmother was very beautiful and intelligent, as she had been at a Grammar School and she would sit with me and help me with my homework. Her first husband had died in the war and she had met my grandfather, Bert, whilst she was hop picking with her family on a farm in Kent where my grandfather worked at that time.

He was tall and blond, very handsome and a lady's man—the sort of man most women would stay away from. He seduced her and got her pregnant, so he did the honourable thing and married her; though he was not in love with her, she was hopelessly in love with him and that was her demise.

My Grandmother Isabella already had a child from her previous marriage—Pat, my aunt was extremely kind and supportive of me whilst growing up.

Isabella ran the home with five children and eight grandchildren and turned a blind eye to my grandfather not coming home or staying out as he was a 'ladies man' true to form.

When my grandfather went bankrupt from having his own business, it was my grandmother who then went and got a job in a toy factory, leaving the house every morning at 7:30. Still, all our uniforms would be pressed and warmed by the fire, our sandwiches would be packed and a hardy breakfast would be served to set us up for the day. My grandmother loved that job and she had—for the first time in her life—freedom, friendship at work and her own money. I loved my grandmother dearly. She did put me on a pedestal and she wanted me to do well and achieve all the things that she dreamed of doing—and I have some but there is so much more to come as I have only really just discovered who I am.

MY MOTHER – ROSEMARY

Though I greatly respect and admire my mother for bringing up 3 children as a single mother due to being widowed at a very young age and she is extremely intelligent and beautiful on the outside to this day because of the rape attack on holiday in 2013 and the lack of support which I feel she as a mother did not and could not offer me when I needed her the most I don't have a relationship with my mother. I do forgive her and have managed to move on which was down to my therapy and I wish her a healthy, happy life.

On holiday in August 2015, returning to that holiday destination, I was asked by my therapist if I could revisit the venue where it all started. I had a few glasses of Prosecco and I did just that. I informed my mother that was my intention and she commented, "Why should you put yourself through this?" I had to be able to move on and had been having panic attacks and I was diagnosed with PTSS. As a Woman Warrior, I walked alone into that bar and ordered a drink and when the Bar Tender/Owner came over who I have known for 15 years he looked straight through me and pretended not to know me, but he did and I asked him politely, how he and his family were? He did not respond. I looked around and noted the Bar was empty and was informed by an Australian mother and daughter having fun together that their music and late night licence was taken away. I was relieved as I was not the only female that had been stalked in that Bar, then had a drug rape substance put in my drink to then be followed back to my hotel and raped and beaten to be hospitalised. I was always under the opinion that the perpetrators were the friends of the DJ and indeed lived with him. The flat where they lived in the Marina was owned by the owners of the Bar.

I am presently undergoing cognitive therapy as I need to become that "Woman Warrior", this time for myself to be brave so I can support and inspire other women. What is worse than rape to me is betrayal and by someone who is supposed to love you unconditionally.

On hearing about this, an ex-friend and lover for many years, Nino, who sadly passed way Summer 2016 said that my attacker 'sleeps with the fishes'. I also heard at the same time that an American girl, attacked like me, through her family and their money, managed to take to court, the rest of the gang from Naples of African descent, refugees. They are now in prison including the woman who aided their evil. I was relieved that no other woman will ever have to go through what I suffered by them, but though Nino's words were the most comforting to me and I am a practicing Christian.

RICHARD BRANSON'S MUM – EVE – EXACTLY HOW GOD INTENDED!

Much has been written about whether entrepreneurs are born or made, with no real consensus. My own opinion, which is anecdotal, is that entrepreneurs can be made and that parents play a central role in making them.

I had a remarkable epiphany while producing *Lemonade Stories,* a documentary film about extraordinary entrepreneurs and their mothers. The film, which features Richard Branson (of Virgin), Russell Simmons (of Def Jam), Arthur Blank (of the Home Depot and owner of the Atlanta Falcons) and Tom Scott (of Nantucket Nectars), among others, examines the impact that mothers have on sparking creativity and entrepreneurial spirit in their children.

During her interview, Eve Branson talked extensively about her son's shyness as a boy, which she described as "disabling." That evening, as my crew sat down to dinner, our director of photography and our gaffer started buzzing about Eve's comments. This was unusual. Normally when filming interviews, my team is focused exclusively on their craft (e.g. the operation and movement of the camera, monitoring of sound levels and positioning of lights) and is not attuned to the actual content of interviews. But I knew we were on to something special when they both described how they might incorporate Eve's advice into how they were raising their own teenage children.

When Richard Branson was a young boy, he refused to talk to adults and would cling to the back of Eve's skirt. When he turned seven or so, Eve decided that his behaviour was no longer tolerable. "Shyness is being introverted and thinking only of yourself," she said. On the way home from a shopping trip to a nearby village, Eve stopped the car about three miles from home and let Richard out. "You will now walk home. You must talk to people to find your way home," she told him. By the time Richard arrived some ten hours later, Eve was apoplectic. (She had not accounted for the time he might stop to look at bugs and inspect rocks.) But it worked. Richard started to become more comfortable interacting with adults.

On my flight, back to the States from London, I thought about my son who, too, was shy. When he shrank back from adults, I would often apologise: "I'm sorry, he's so shy." Until my conversation with Eve, it had never occurred to me that being shy was being selfish. When Eve put shyness into that context, I decided that this trait would now have a very short shelf life in our household.

I began Project Stick-Out-Your-Hand-and-Look-People-in-the-Eye. And my son, who was seven years old at the time, very quickly learned that there was a significant upside to interacting with adults and making them feel comfortable—like new sunglasses on his birthday from the couple down the street. Now, at the age of fifteen, my son operates like a senator, looking adults in the eye and shaking their hand. It is a lesson that will serve him well as an adult—and one that I wished I had learned early on.

What a truly inspirational woman. Richard, you are so lucky.

Based on what I learned from the mothers in *Lemonade Stories*, it occurs to me that if American parents want to raise children who think entrepreneurially, have initiative and become innovative and truly independent adults, it might serve us all well if we step back and let our sweet darlings make mistakes and fall on their faces from time to time.

I feel personally indebted to the Eve Branson's of this world—women who taught their children to be independent and gave them space to experiment, to fail. Russell Simmons' mother gave him a $2,000 loan when no one else would; his business of producing parties hosted by rap artists was losing money and he was questioning his ability and line of work. He said in his interview for the film that what was important was not the money his mother gave him, but rather what it represented: the faith that she had in him. After that day, he never had to ask his mother for money again.

I have fallen so flat on my face since I was a child and will keep falling, but I get up a lot quicker now. And instead of feeling beaten and accepting defeat, I smile, as I am happy to challenge again.

UNIT 7

YOUNG WOMEN WARRIORS THAT I HAVE MENTORED WHO HAVE OVERCOME BARRIERS

I HAVE MENTORED SO MANY women entrepreneurs over the years and wanted to share some of their journeys and those who are Women Warriors in different ways – this young lady not only within her career of Law but in Sport paves the way for younger women to have that balance.

SHARON AMESU – MENTEE – BARRISTER – MOTHER AND WIFE – A TRUE WOMAN WARRIOR

I first had the pleasure and honour to meet Sharon whilst she was attending the Women's Organisation in Liverpool. Having had her family members on many of my programs, whom I had mentored, she asked to attend my Work and Business Club ILM Level 7 with her husband Sefa in December 2014. They were an absolute joy and inspiration to work with and because of their hard work, Sharon and her husband raised the bar for me and my mentors; we were supposed to be delivering an ILM Level 5 Leadership and Management and we ended up achieving a Level 7. I knew from the first day that I met Sharon that she was going to make a huge difference. In her former career path as a barrister, Sharon became disillusioned when she felt that she

was not empowering those women from situations like domestic abuse, and so she chose to become a life coach. Sharon has started delivering workshops for women in the Manchester, UK area around confidence-building and assertiveness and I know that she has chosen the right path and that many women and girls will benefit from her gift. Sharon is another Woman Warrior I have the pleasure to know and will hopefully work with soon again.

SHARON'S STORY

I grew up in Manchester in the UK during the 1980s. It was a time of tremendous civil unrest and social disquiet within the BME community for many reasons. My dad was a social activist during this time and he, alongside other prominent people in my community, were becoming figureheads and using their voices to speak up and speak out for those who were experiencing social injustices. I believe that as a BME woman, this where my passion for justice and empowering others stemmed from. By the age of fourteen, I had made a clear and concrete resolution that I wanted to practise law.

I was very blessed in that I had the encouragement and support of the important people in my life. I also had the privilege of meeting incredible people who created extraordinary opportunities for me to pursue and fulfil my dream of practising as a criminal barrister, which I could do for sixteen years. For several of those years, I was appointed Specialist Domestic Violence Prosecutor, where I had the opportunity to work with many women from different walks of life who had been affected by domestic violence.

However, around twelve years into practice, I began to experience a sense of uneasiness about my work. I increasingly began to feel that in relation to domestic violence cases, my role within the criminal justice system could sometimes be disempowering toward women. This would mostly be where (as was frequently the case) a victim would decide that she didn't wish to proceed with a prosecution; I would be a part of the process that would necessarily take the decision out of her hands and compel her to attend court. However, after the court process was complete, irrespective of the outcome, I would often see a woman leave the court building feeling voiceless, unsupported and even emasculated.

It was also around this time that I was introduced to Personal Development Coaching. Here I experienced first-hand how powerful coaching could be in altering the vision and the trajectory of one's life. I was hooked and knew that somehow I wanted to use my knowledge, skills and experiences from the Bar and merge it with coaching skills to help other women and empower them from within.

I trained as a Personal Development Coach and Trainer and soon began to coach a few clients and deliver a few training sessions. I was thrilled to hear clients stating that they were experiencing real results and changes in their lives. From this point, I knew that I wanted to make a difference in people's lives in this very positive way. In June of 2014, having straddled two professions for two years, I finally decided to take the leap, leave the Bar and set up my company, Life in Colour Ltd. It was a huge and significant step outside of a comfort zone, which I had been settled in for so long; however, the journey has been and continues to be exhilarating. I'm now working with a whole range of organisations, schools and women in business, delivering cutting-edge personal development coaching and training. I've also met some incredibly inspirational and pioneering women warriors along the way who have exemplified the power of sheer grit and determination. My hope is that I can do the same for other women and girls and pass on a baton of hope, aspiration and fulfilment of purpose.

Sharon Amesu

Director of Life in Colour Ltd.

I feel sure that Sharon and I will work together on many projects for the future.

UNIT 8

8 MARCH 2015 – INTERNATIONAL WOMEN'S DAY

IN 2015, I DID NOT DO much to support International Women's Day, as I had just returned from working in London for the week and it was hectic preparing to open my new office in London in June. I was signing up new partners, networking and shooting a video for a Chinese International Mentoring Platform for Rockstar Group—and not once did I go shopping. I returned late to my four-star hotel one evening after finishing my last appointment; I found myself in a lift to the fifth floor with a young Asian male who had had one too many. It started with the leering, then the suggestion of a drink in his room, then the moving forward. I put my hand up to push him away and firmly stated, "No, thank you."

Once I found myself in my room, not having known if I would make it without being attacked in the lift or corridor, I fell on the bed crying. I researched it and it was a sign of POST-TRAUMATIC SHOCK. I was not going to let this silly young man take away my power, so the following morning I was up—I had my workout done and was ready to do business by 7 a.m.

I am not everyone's cup of tea or, indeed, flavour—I do sometimes intend to be "Marmite," but I like to think of myself as "Tutti Frutti"! As I can be nuts at times.

So, what made the news? The feminist site FEMSPLAN was attacked and down for seven hours; China detained Feminine Activists and all those famous stars could not miss a PR opportunity to get in on the act. I will leave you to figure out what it means:

"The story of women's struggle for equality belongs to no single feminist nor to any one organisation but to the collective efforts of all who care about human equality."

International Women's Day March 8 2017 – Launch22 Liverpool

I was very honoured to be invited to be a Guest Speaker at the above. Even though I was booked for London for a Fintech Event I felt it was my duty to support this day. So blessed that God gives me the stage to hopefully change women's lives by empowering them with skills and knowledge and confidence.

TESTIMONIALS

Thank you for such an inspirational presentation yesterday at launch 22 for me personally you managed restore some seeds of doubt I was having in regards to my own entrepreneurship and also for my partner I know you have inspired in her that such things are even a possibility. I particularly appreciated how honest and Frank you where in regards to your personal demons and hoped you may be able to assist with my company that wishes to help others do the same Www.recoveryinc.co.uk thanks for your time on this kindest regards DS

Hi there. I was at your talk today at Launch 22 and was really inspired! Regards, D

I was inspired by not only the women but the men in the room. Especially, Dawn's comments as I awoke the following morning having lost a big contract and was not feeling the love but when you have beautiful, encouraging, comments like this it makes my work all the more worthwhile – if I change one person's life in a group – then I have done my job and achieved Purpose.!

UNIT 9

GENDER PAY GAP AND THE NUMBER OF WOMEN ON BOARDS WITHIN THE UK

Labour Politician Yvette Cooper has been asking the government to consider introducing quotas for the number of women on corporate boards in the UK. In addition, bringing in a new Equalities Act would push for free childcare for three- and four-year-olds and the proper living wage to benefit careers. This is reported in citam.com as a Feminist Campaign.

I believe if you are meant to be a board member, you will get there on merit and not just because you are ticking a box for the government's legislation. As for equal pay, it goes without saying that you should be paid the same amount as your male counterpart.

The www.fawcettsociety.or.uk Report 2015 below:

In modern Britain, despite the 1970 Equal Pay Act, women still earn less than men. The gender pay gap remains the clearest and most dramatic example of economic inequality for women today.

The overall pay gap stands at 19.1 percent (2014), measured by median gross hourly pay. Whilst the gap has fallen significantly from 27.5 percent in 1997, this figure is still above the EU 2014 average of 16.4 percent, a range that includes Slovenia at 3.2 percent and Estonia at 29.9 percent.

Equity brings Diversity! Women's Event Liverpool IFB2016 Guest Speaker for Forward Ladies and Innovate UK

The pay gaps vary between men and women in different groups, such as age, education and employment and some women earn a similar amount to their male equivalents, but many more earn less. Lower earnings over a lifetime usually lead to lower savings, smaller pensions and less economic independence than men.

This gap has several main causes.

THE MOTHERHOOD PENALTY

Women are far more likely to work part-time than full-time, due to childcare responsibilities. Part-time work is typically lower-skill and pays less per hour than full-time work. Whilst women as a group earn on average 19.1 percent less than men as a group, women in full-time jobs earn 9.4 percent less than other men in full-time work.

Young women from eighteen to thirty-nine in full-time work experience a very low or even reversed gender pay gap. The gap for hourly earnings opens from the age of forty onwards, as women begin taking time out of the labour market to have children. On return to work, reduced opportunities for career progression can force women to take up less senior and lower-paid roles.

When women make the choice to reduce their hours to begin taking care of their children, they are sacrificing not just their current income but their future income too.

CONCENTRATION IN LOW-WAGE SECTORS (OCCUPATIONAL SEGREGATION)

Stereotypes around men and women's roles and value in the workplace still exist. Jobs traditionally carried out by women, such as cleaning and catering, are typically undervalued and paid less than jobs traditionally done by men, such as construction and engineering.

78% of those working in health and social care, a low-paid sector, are women; 88% of those working in STEM (Science, Technology, Engineering and Mathematics) industries, a high-paid sector, are men.

The recovery has seen a growth in low-wage "feminised" sectors and occupational segregation could prove to be a persistent obstacle to future reductions to the gender pay gap. Overall, 62% of workers paid below the Living Wage (set at £8.25) are women.

The effect is more marked for older women, who are less likely to have university educations than men of the same age, leading to lower earnings relative to men of the same age.

OUTRIGHT DISCRIMINATION

Over the forty years since the Dagenham machinists took action that led to the introduction of the Equal Pay Act, direct and indirect discrimination against women persists in the workplace. Direct discrimination occurs when individuals are paid different amounts for the same job and indirect discrimination occurs when they are paid different amounts for work of "equivalent value." Both forms of discrimination are illegal and employees can seek redress through the legal system.

These factors contribute to a shocking level of economic inequality between women and men: The means gender pay gap for full-time employees currently stands at 15.7%. This means that over the course of a year women effectively stop earning, relative to men, on 4 November— this day is referred to as Equal Pay Day.

WHAT WE WANT TO SEE HAPPEN

Tackling the gender pay gap will require concerted action on several fronts:

- Expanding opportunities for quality flexible and part-time work—employers can benefit from a diverse workforce and a retention of talent.
- Improving rules on parental leave—it needs to be more financially rewarding to encourage men to take up more childcare.

- Lifting the national minimum wage—this would benefit all workers on low pay, but particularly women, as they are most those on low pay.
- Challenging stereotypes to encourage men and women to enter jobs that are outside stereotypical gender roles.
- Seeing the gap—despite a government scheme to encourage large companies to publish salaries, April 2015 had seen only five large employers conducting and publishing gender pay audits. We're calling for other parties to match the Liberal Democrats' pledge of an enactment of section 78 of the 2010 Equality Act, which makes gender pay audits mandatory for large employers (250+ employees).

EQUAL PAY

I could not leave this subject out since Patricia Arquette demanded Equal Pay and Rights for Women at the Oscars in February 2015.

Here it goes:

"To every woman who gave birth, to every taxpayer and citizen of this nation, we have fought for everybody else's equal rights. It's our time to have wage equality once and for all and equal rights for women in the United States of America."

CASE STUDY – STEPHANIE WRIGHT LIVERPOOL 2014

In 2014 I had the pleasure to meet a young lady with a family in Liverpool who came to me for support on starting a women's only support for business. At our first meeting, I thought, 'h*ere we go again. She has good intentions, but I am not being drawn back to doing the legwork and then being left holding the baby—been there and done that*'. Then we were both speakers at the International Business Event in Liverpool and I noted that when she spoke, though nervous, she had a certain innocence about her that touched me. Then we eventually had a coffee in October 2014 and though I had only intended to give her an hour of my time, we ended up speaking for three hours. I could feel her pain as well as her passion and enthusiasm, and so began our journey. These are Steph's words, which are raw but true and said from the heart:

I am Liverpool-born, but I was raised in Ottawa until I was about eight years old. My parents separated and my mum brought my brother and me back to Liverpool. Almost overnight, my father and his family in Canada, who we had been very close to, washed their hands of us. Contact was and still is very sporadic, but the older I have become, the less it troubles me. In many ways, the hurt I felt as a little girl was masked by the influx of my mum's family, who we became very close to very quickly.

In 1989, my world was rocked forever. Everything about me—who I was, how I saw the world, how I did things—changed irreversibly when my big cousin Simon went to a football match in Sheffield and never came home.

I am a survivor not a victim of Domestic abuse and now support others to become free and confident and take ownership of their beautiful lives that we all deserve.

I have always been a happy soul, no matter what life has thrown at me. I like to think I see the positives even though they may appear faint. I have been through a lot, faced many heartbreaks and situations that might have broken some people, but I am stubborn and determined too. I am a mum of three; I am strong and I am blessed.

Now I am an entrepreneur who works with women, helping them get set up as entrepreneurs and helping them face their demons in the process. I know now that my experiences in life have enriched me and make me a better mentor to the women I help. I understand the barriers women face, I know how their experiences can knock their confidence and because of that, I can help them rebuild their strength.

We have become great friends and in a way, I mentor Steph and will continue to support her so that she is able to share her newfound inner strength to support her daughters to become Women Warriors, whether in business, education, or life. Steph is just beginning her journey and I am honoured for her to have chosen me to come along for the ride.

UNIT 10

WOMEN WARRIORS TAKE ON THE "HAPPY ENTREPRENEUR MINDSET"

I WAS READING THE BOOK *In Search of the Woman Warrior* by Richard J Lane and Jay Wurts whilst on a chill break with my BBF Sheila—it explores the Amazons and the modern Amazons. As an example, under King Charles's reign, Molly Frith was a "land-locked privateer," and though she dressed as a man and had the courage of a man, I do not feel that imitating men is necessary to be a successful entrepreneur. The book goes on to discuss 'RADIGUNDS' one being Edith who went on to run her own business for grant proposals for mental health etc. Edith searched for role models and found these in Eleanor Roosevelt and what I observed is that with power comes conflict and then you don't become that 'HAPPY ENTREPRENEUR' or have that mindset—so I would not want any greater power than to inspire and motivate other entrepreneurs to become successful.

An example of a Woman Warrior who has overcome so much is Alison Abruneiras, a survivor of cancer.

Thousands of Brits have turned to eBay to save or make a few pounds—but not many can say that it has helped them to make a fortune.

Alison Abruneiras runs a successful business grossing more than £1 million a year after becoming addicted to the auction website. Incredibly, the 46-year-old mum left school with no qualifications or business experience.

Alison was making just £70 a week as a nail technician when breast cancer forced her to stop working altogether. But, after logging onto eBay in her bedroom at home as a fun "hobby" to take her mind off the treatment, she's become a hugely successful entrepreneur.

In six years, her cosmetic retail business, the Nail and Beauty Emporium, has grown to become a big hit on eBay. It now trades worldwide and Alison has had to expand into a warehouse and take on four staff—including her 22-year-old daughter, Coralia, who is set to take over the business.

Alison, from Lincoln, said:

Looking back, it's incredible to think that this all started with my computer in my bedroom. It has been hard work, but I'd like to show other people that it can be done—if I can do it, anyone can. Anyone can earn money. You don't have to have an education; I don't have a GCSE to my name.

Alison has had an interest in business since childhood. At eleven years old, she was given a little market stall by her shopkeeper dad to sell washing-up liquid and other small items, but she never pursued her talent.

At the age of 21, she moved to Lanzarote, Spain, after falling in love with her now-husband Amador, 47 and worked as a holiday rep and nail technician.

The couple had their children Coralia, Amador, 21 and Luis, 15, before moving back to the UK in 2005 where Alison continued work as a nail technician. At the age of 38, she was forced to give it up after being diagnosed with breast cancer.

For the next two years, she underwent agonising treatment, including a lumpectomy and mastectomy. Her ovaries and lymph nodes were removed before she began a course of chemotherapy.

"It was a huge shock to me," Alison said. "When you're diagnosed with something like that, it knocks you off your feet. I lost a lot of my confidence and became incredibly depressed."

With spare time on her hands, Alison turned her attention to eBay. She explained:

I didn't want my whole world and life to be about cancer and chemo and that's how I discovered eBay—I wanted a hobby. I needed something to take me away from that hell, something to focus on—eBay, at the time, was my focus and it was exciting.

I started by buying a foot spa from an end-of-line shop and seeing if I could sell it for a profit. I bought it for £10 and within a week I'd sold it for £30. I would be checking the Internet every half an hour. Making that sale gave me that buzz and made me feel good. I didn't think about whether I was going to die or whether the treatment was going to work.

Everything was a real whirlwind, but building my business gave me a way of fighting cancer. Then, when I'd finished the treatment, I was left with an empty void and I was wondering what I was going to do next. That's when my business took off; I put everything into it after that.

Boosted by her new-found sales talent, Alison used her expertise as a nail technician to expand into other cosmetic products: "I bought £3,000 worth of products from a wholesaler and stored them in my bedroom, which had become my office. Within two weeks I'd nearly sold all of that too. From there it became an addiction—I'd be on the computer first thing in the morning and up until midnight."

The business proved a real lifeline when Amador lost his job as a restaurant manager in 2010.

Alison said, "My hobby suddenly became the only income and I knew we were going to have to make it a success to survive. Amador started working with me and we worked together for two years. He put some really good things in place and we made it work."

Three years ago, Alison went from sole trader to a limited company and today her business continues to boom, expanding to the websites Amazon and Play.

But, despite all her success, she remains incredibly grounded and lives a modest lifestyle. At her three-bedroom rented home, you won't find designer clothes and flashy cars. In fact, the only luxuries Alison enjoys are family holidays to Florida and Egypt and a brand-new camper van.

She's also treated Coralia to a brand-new Mini as a reward for working so hard. She said, *"My daughter has taken a leaf out of my book—like me, she didn't do very well at school and left with no qualifications. But she's proving a real whizz when it comes to business—everything she knows is self-taught. She's amazing on social media and all the suppliers love her."*

Alison has now set her sights on the hospitality industry and has opened a Spanish tapas restaurant, called Ole Ole, next door to the family home. Under the management of Amador, it has also become a huge success in just five months—already rated fifth best of 335 restaurants in Lincoln on TripAdvisor.

Alison concluded, *"We have worked like crazy and life has completely changed, but it's changed for the better."*

I can relate to this, Alison overcame adversity and turned a negative into a positive. What started out as a hobby she has turned into a million-pound business. Not only that, but she is self-taught; she never gave up and always believed in herself, though not educated. What I love about Alison is that she then went on to support her husband, who himself was made redundant and faced uncertainty in the future.

I was not so long ago faced with another failing business, poor health and the need to turn my business around to support my mother, who had breast cancer. Then to top it all, my husband was made redundant after a serious accident at work and we had to downsize and move home to support my mother. It took me eighteen months to support my husband to find a new career. He started out as a kitchen porter with a famous restaurant chain and is now on their Head Chef Academy. I, no doubt, will be supporting him to start his own Italian restaurant. I never gave up believing in myself and others never stopped believing in me. So, thank you to my husband, friends and colleagues who supported me through this challenging time.

Women Warriors such as Nicola Horlick have paved the way through crowdfunding, rather than the intimidating platform of the Dragons' Den. Women can use it in the comfort of their own homes, instead of rocking up to a VC Angels Pitch, paying for the privilege and then facing an all-male panel to be humiliated.

Investing often used to seem like a closed shop—the preserve of a wealthy, privileged elite keeping business opportunities all to itself.

Now technology has blown open the doors and given everyone—not just the professional investors and big institutions—a chance to get a piece of the action.

Would-be Warren Buffets can go online and buy shares in start-ups and early stage companies for as little as £10.

But while there's a chance you could be backing the next Google, Apple, or Facebook, there's also a strong risk you could end up losing all your money.

ONLINE DRAGON'S DEN

This is the world of crowd investing, also known as equity crowdfunding.

The difference with other forms of crowdfunding is that you're not lending money in return for interest on the loan, or donating money in return for rewards and perks, you're buying a slice of the company.

Typically, firms seeking a cash injection upload their business plans, including how much they're hoping to raise and how much of their business they're prepared to sell and at what price.

Think of it like an online Dragons' Den involving hundreds of investors rather than a handful of Dragons.

I have the pleasure of working with Nicola again at the World Festival of Female Entrepreneurs Bristol UK on October 22, 2015, supporting women to stand up and come forward with their ideas of great businesses.

UNIT 11

EXECUTIVE LEADERSHIP – CAREER PROGRESSION

I deliver in the UK Leadership and Management courses to Level 7, at my Work and Business Club in Warrington Cheshire for David Mowat MP for Warrington South. David wrote the original Job Club Manual *Get Britain Working* at the start of the recession 2007 for professionals as endorsed by Theresa May MP. I have since gone on to write and deliver *Fast Track to Success*, turned into a book in 2014 for Hope University Liverpool and delivered for DWPJCP/PERA/Department of Innovation and Skills. I first started working in this arena in 2000 in London, delivering career progression programs for top FTSE companies, from Price Waterhouse to Kleinwort Benson, from Academia to Guildhall University and LETECT Careers.

On that note, I am supporting Sharon to stage the biggest women's event in October 2015 in Manchester and have asked another Woman Warrior, Lindsey Sharratt, to share this stage with us.

LINDSEY SHARRATT TRANSFORMATIONAL COACH – WOMAN WARRIOR

BIOGRAPHY – Lindsey's background in corporate IT has given her both a first-hand understanding of the problems that women face when pursuing a management career and a passion for helping women worldwide achieve career success to the highest level. Her own observations from managing staff have reinforced her belief that a female style of management—collaborative, empathic, inclusive and environmental—is enormously beneficial to companies and that encouraging and assisting women to achieve on a large scale is of benefit, not only to her clients but to their employers too. Her studies and research during her Psychology degree have given her a greater understanding of the ways in which women can be held back from these levels of success and how they can work to overcome these challenges. In addition to coaching, Lindsey is the author of *It's All in Your Mind*, which deals with the psychology behind how we learn and develop and how we can use the same techniques to reprogram our minds to overcome unhelpful conditioning, negative beliefs and trauma. Lindsey is available to speak at conferences worldwide. Her material is relevant to a wide variety of audiences but can be tailored to specific requirements. Her specialist areas are:

- empowerment strategies for female executives and professionals
- corporate team building and leadership skills
- personal development and overcoming psychological blocks.

I first came across Lindsey on LinkedIn in female entrepreneur groups, we arranged a conference call and discovered that Lindsey was hosting a Women's Warrior Conference in Miami. I asked her to support us, with Sharon, hosting in the UK in 2015. Lindsey also joined me as a coach on my former business www.workbizacademy.co.uk.

I met Karen through our shared passion for helping women to fulfil their career and business ambitions. Karen has a vast amount of senior management and business experience and a real empathy for the issues that face women who aspire to reach the highest levels. She understands exactly what it takes to get to the top and the different pressures that women face in roles that are more frequently held by men. She has an ongoing commitment to seeing women achieve big in career and business and an impressive degree of skill to support them in doing so.

I am privileged to have been invited to work with Karen in 2015. My own field is the use of psychology to challenge the personal and social stereotypes that face women who follow non-traditional, executive career paths and reinforcement of the value of female personality traits and leadership ability. I look forward to being able to assist Karen in supporting women to take up their power, increase their confidence and bring their unique skills to senior management

LEADERSHIP – IS A PROCESS THROUGH TRANSITIONAL SKILLS

Leaders commonly face several major types of transitions in their careers. Each of these requires an adjustment in behaviours, capabilities, attitudes and thinking. Some of these major transitional challenges are described below.

Change in job/role. I have noted a change in my leadership skills in being the CEO/Chairman of my companies and managing a small team of all men who are mature in years but highly experienced. It has been challenging and they have resisted at times my decisions but 3 years' later most are still with me as we learn together and grow together. I though was told in Jan 2017 that I need to retune my listening skills and learn to trust more. I have now moved into a new phase of Leadership/management as I know have a lead Investor/NED/Chairman to be and having to listen to his requests and act quickly to his demands and deliver goal orientated tasks is within my comfort zone but just sometimes I want to do it 'my way'.

Change in people. Sometimes the people we work with change jobs. Working with different bosses, peers and subordinates is an important transition and one in which leaders must ride the waves. Learning to interact productively with new people who have diverse ideas, styles and preferences is a difficult challenge. While learning, such lessons seem basic, many leaders fail to navigate people changes—particularly when they get a new boss like we have for 2017.

Change in the marketplace. Markets change in many ways and leaders who are effective in transitions pay attention to these market changes. They understand the need to keep abreast of the business, industry and marketplace trends. They do not take things for granted. When we launched in 2014 we were a Fintech Alternative Finance platform only one of 3 into the UK now that this market is saturated we enter 2017 as a new Company structure in a new marketplace as a membership hub for our strong 770000 members to buy and sell – exchange ideas – recruit

– learn – post events etc and only work in Finance/Investment sourcing and planning with a new Chairman to be.

Change in strategy/products. Often in response to the competitive environment, firms will look at changing their strategy and/or their product mix. Leaders must adjust their organisational thinking and way of doing business when the enterprise shifts direction. Yet many leaders have difficulty making this transition.

Leaders who successfully embrace this type of change become the enablers or the people who help promote, accept and make the change happen. The organisation values these types of leaders because they ensure strategic growth.

On the other hand, it is difficult for the organisation when leaders become "open resistors" to the change or actively work against the changes. They may engage in activities such as sabotaging change efforts, promoting to keep things the same, arguing openly against the changes in meetings, or creating coalitions to fight the change effort. They can also become "nay-sayers" or openly criticise the changes and those involved in it. Leaders who are not successfully transitioning possibly become "passive resistors" or privately refuse to support the change, though they do not overtly resist the change. However, they also do not do anything to enable the change. Finally, some individuals might be unwary resistors or not be aware that they are resisting the change effort. They simply revert to what they know, which could be old processes, old priorities and old strategies.

So, for me, I am having to retrain my brain to leave behind my old 'mindset' or doing the business of corporate 90's to being in the 21st century as my new Chairman to be is only 32 and male and a tech wizard brought up on digital marketing and all that is digital.

HOW TRANSITIONS IMPACT A LEADER'S PERFORMANCE AS A LEADER I LEARNT HOW TO RIDE OUT THE CHANGES TO STAY AHEAD.

1. Staying ahead – I am this type of LEADER that recognises points at which to make the transition to stay ahead and take full advantage of the opportunities.
2. Keeping up – This type of LEADER can sometimes dip in performance but then gathers confidence and information to then peak. So sometimes, or in the beginning they miss the transition point.
3. Falling behind – These LEADERS do not recognise Transition points and thus fall way behind and thus fail to become a fully fledged leader.
4. There is a 4th level where the Leader becomes the Entrepreneur within an organisation which is now encouraged within major large Fintech companies and I know that the culture within say for example VIRGIN is to encourage their employees to bring their innovation to Management to implement within the organisation and even encourage the employee to leave and start their own business.

COMPANY RESPONSES TO LEADERSHIP TRANSITIONS

It is extremely expensive and disruptive for an organisation to see leaders fail or to have leaders who are ill equipped for their positions. Thus, companies are beginning to recognise how critical it is to help their leaders make a transition through the more difficult situations.

I would not personally work within an organisation that that did encourage Mentoring/Coaching from within and normally this is having Management leading in this role to mentor younger and new employees who have joined the company to facilitate career advancement more quickly and that is transparent.

INDIVIDUAL TRANSITION SKILLS NEEDED

WHILE ORGANISATIONS FACILITATE THIS PROCESS IT IS INVIDUALUALS THAT ARE THE DRIVER OF THIS PROCESS.

SUCCESSFUL LEADERS CAN CHANGE THEIR BEHAVIOUR TO SUIT THE TRANSITION NEEDED.

Perhaps one or more areas in the characteristics of the Leader needs to change. Sometimes, the employee will become bored within the process and move on to take on new challenges. .

SPECIFIC STEPS

HOW WELL DO YOU NAVIAGATE TRANSITIONAL SKILLS?

NOT JUST AT WORK BUT ALL AROUND YOU – HOME – ENVIRONMENT

CAN LEADERSHIP BE LEARNT THROUGH LEARN-ING?

TAKE A LOOK IN THE MIRROR AND ASK YOURSELF THE QUESTION? ARE YOU A BORN LEADER? ARE YOU WORKING ON YOUR TRANSITIONAL POINTS TO BECOME ONE? OR IS IT A TASK IN PROGRESS?

YOU CAN HAVE ONE TO ONE COACHING AND

FEEDBACK IS ALWAYS WELCOMED BY PEOPLE YOU ADMIRE AS LEADERS. YOU WILL GET THERE FASTER WITH A COACH/MENTOR.

IT IS ALL ABOUT REFLECTION TO MOVE FORWARD TO TAKE CONTROL OF THE TRANSITION TO BECOME THAT EFFECTIVE LEADER.

LEARNING AND EVEN MODELLING YOURSELF ON LEADERS YOU ADMIRE – WATCH THEIR BODY LANGUAGE – THEIR LANGUAGE – DRESS – AND EVEN WHO THEY HANG OUT WITH.

IN ORDER TO BE COMPETITIVE IN YOUR OWN INDUSTRY OR ENVIRONMENT – DO YOU REALLY KNOW AND UNDERSTAND IT?

GREAT LEADERS KNOW THEY CANNOT MAKE IT ON THEIR OWN AND ALWAYS HAVE EVEN A GREATER TEAM AROUND THEM.

IN YOUR BUSINESS DO YOU KNOW IT INSIDE OUT?

Business Acumen – The development of a deeper understanding of the business so that you understand how the business is changing and why and how you might need to change as a leader.

- Do you proactively seek to know more about the business so that you can help move it in the direction it needs to go?
- Do you pay attention to industry trends, market trends and strategic shifts that are taking place?
- Do you apply these trends to how you might need to change as a leader?

- Does your company embrace Entrepreneurship within your organisation? Create new projects within your organisation that inspire and motivate your employees ENTRAPEURSHIP.

MODERN LEADERSHIP AND MANAGEMENT SKILLS – TRANSITIONAL SKILLS

RESEARCH – your skills – the skills of the team and the culture of the Organisation

PLANNING – within your role develop your role – Appraisal JD

LISTENING – using your Emotional Intelligence to listen to all

EMPLOYEE ENGAGEMENT – work alongside as part of the Team and learn

You may not be in a role that requires leadership skills, but if you have identified your TRANSFERABLE SKILLS, then you can recognise and develop them, which then would give you tools to use CHANGE MANAGEMENT SKILLS within an organisation normally when a crisis arises. Remember what type of management style you would apply:

PREDICTIVE

REACTIVE or a combination of both?

COACHING

Some organisations use Transitional Coaching as a method to train new management to achieve quick results and success and to prepare managers for leadership leading to promotion.

The purpose of this workshop is for you to understand your transferable skills, to navigate your way through the changes within your organisation or when you join a new organisation—each step is a transition and you must MANAGE this journey.

As a LEADER, you will adapt your expertise to acquire new skills to face the challenges of the role.

For example: Write down what you learned in week 12 on this Program Level 5/7 on this Leadership and Management ILM Program for Executives into Work. This is part of the NHS Model for Search and Selection—this manual will support you through the twists and turns of your new role.

Agility and adaptability are mandatory these days, as leaders prepare, manage and sometimes reinvent themselves to navigate the twists, turns and transitions they must make. Otherwise, making the wrong move could eventually scuttle a once-promising leadership career.

"All things change; nothing abides. Into the same river, one cannot step twice"

— Heraclitus

How well we manage these changes within our role at work will determine those who will be successful and those who will fail. Many points in our jobs and careers require, even demand, changes in our leadership behaviours, competencies, attitudes and thinking. How well we navigate these potentially treacherous junctures often determines our ultimate success—or failure—as leaders.

This is where it will become obvious to your peers and to you if you are a leader or manager or both. You can, of course, evolve. What are you? What changes have you made since being on this program? What do you want to be? Why? Now list your:

COMPETENCIES – SKILLS

MINDSET – Are you in the right frame to take this on?

APPLICATION – Are you ready to apply yourself?

BEHAVIOUR – Are you displaying to your team and peers that you are ready and ABLE?

CHANGE

Whether change involves the strategic direction of the corporation, a merger, acquisition or reorganisation, the development of a new product line or a shift in the competitive marketplace, or new bosses or co-workers, leaders must constantly monitor their environment and adjust their leadership skills to match the new demands. This requirement for constant personal modification can be daunting for anyone not agile enough to adapt.

It is imperative that leaders determine how they need to adjust their leadership behaviours and style to navigate the changes surrounding them. This task sounds easy, but it is often very difficult.

TACTICS TO MANOEUVRE CHANGE USING YOUR TRANSITIONAL SKILLS

Don't rely on past behaviours to take you through—they won't

Personal changes will be required—sacrifices

If you don't change—you will be forced to leave

ROLEPLAY EXAMPLE

Company takeover – Now your company is focused on outcome-driven performance and you must report and be accountable to someone above you; before, you were only accountable to yourself and your team and you decided on what the outcomes would be. Different culture – How long do you think you must change and fit in?

From coping with the mastering Transitional Skills, you will be valued more to employers and will see in yourself the rewards and have a higher value of yourself.

EXAMPLE – RON PARKER, VICE PRESIDENT HR PEPSICO

Ron Parker, executive vice president of Human Resources at PepsiCo, notes that successful leaders must be "learning agile." "You have to be agile in your approach to complex issues," he says. Parker indicates that corporations need people who can change with the times. "You cannot stay in a steady state in a competitive global environment. That which is not broken today should be broken tomorrow. We look at the entire value chain and are constantly asking ourselves what needs to change." Leaders need to be asking themselves the same questions: How and what do I need to change to keep up with the future and to be of value to this organisation?

PERSONAL VIEW POINT

I have noted of late that many organisations are now looking for entrepreneur/enterprising skills in leaders of today and I am not convinced of this – again depending on the culture of the Company.

Dear Fellow Leaders and Managers,

Are you a good leader?

I am sure you will answer "yes" to that question, but are you 100% confident that your team would agree?

Below is **a checklist of fifteen qualities of good leaders**. If you can be honest with yourself, this test will tell you how a good a leader you are so you can work on the areas where you fall short.

ARE YOU A GOOD LEADER? TAKE THE TEST NOW

To get maximum benefit from this, you need to be 100% honest with yourself. Ready? Here goes:

1. Leaders without a vision will fail

Leaders need to align the organisation around a clear and achievable vision. Without it, they will fail to inspire or motivate teams.

2. Leaders need character and integrity

Regardless of how intelligent, knowledgeable, or persuasive they are, if a leader has a habit of rationalising unethical behaviour, they will fail themselves eventually.

3. Poor performance signals poor leadership

As Myatt says, "Nobody is perfect, but leaders who consistently fail are not leaders, no matter how much you wish they were."

4. Are you a know-it-all?

According to Myatt, "The best leaders are acutely aware of how much they don't know. They have no need to be the smartest person in the room, but have the unyielding desire to learn from others."

5. Communication skills are essential

Leaders need to be able to convey their message effectively and enlighten those who "don't get it."

6. Leaders must understand the concept of "service above self"

Ego, pride and arrogance are not desirable leadership traits. Good leaders take the blame and give credit.

7. Great leaders have empathy, humility and kindness

These traits should not be regarded as weaknesses in any circumstances.

8. "One size fits all" leadership doesn't work

"The best leaders are fluid and flexible in their approach," insists Myatt. "They understand the power of and the necessity for, contextual leadership."

9. Leaders who lack discipline set a bad example

Focus and attention to detail are essential and intentions must be aligned with results.

10. Leaders must relinquish their comfort zone

Being satisfied with the status quo won't bring about growth or innovation.

11. The consumer needs attention

Leaders must be attuned to the market and focus on the customer experience.

12. Leaders must invest in their team

"The best leaders support their team, build into their team, mentor and coach their team and they truly care for their team," says Myatt.

13. Leaders must be accountable

They shouldn't try to pass the buck for failures that occur on their watch.

14. Culture matters

Culture shouldn't evolve by itself—it should be designed. Have you created a positive culture in your team?

15. Leaders need courage

Myatt explains: "Courage is having the strength of conviction to do the right thing when it would just be easier to do things right."

THREE THINGS YOU MUST DO WHEN INNOVATION GOES WRONG

How do you deal with failure? Say, your start-up company flounders, or your new product flops, or you simply get fired?

1. Acknowledge sadness

When you envision a golden future that doesn't become a reality, it's natural to feel sadness. Johnson says it's important to grieve, insisting that sublimating sadness risks the loss of one's passion, which is "an essential lubricant for the engine of innovation."

2. Don't be ashamed

You shouldn't let the failure define you, or "the millstone of shame will drown you and your dreams."

Johnson explains: "According to the ground-breaking research of shame and vulnerability expert Dr Brené Brown, this is especially acute for those involved in professional sports, the military and corporate life."

3. Learn the right lesson

Johnson takes inspiration from the author J. K. Rowling, who said: "Rock bottom became the solid foundation upon which I rebuilt my life."

FAILURE OR SUCCESS

To achieve success, you must have gone through the painful process of failure/s. You can still dream and this is part of the process of achieving success. I have had many failures and successes and I do not at my mature age measure my success now by pounds but by what makes me happy and what I can give to others so that they can become successful in their careers.

In 2014 I started a new business, www.gateway2enterprise.co.uk, an alternative comparison site for finance for businesses to start and grow. There have been "duvet" days when I have wanted to throw in the towel, but I have not and will not, as I know that success comes with hard work and belief. One of my highlights this year was one of my mentees, Babz at FreshRB, who overcome cancer whilst starting and growing a business. Seeing him develop and tearing up when he praised my support on social media—that is a success to me!

BE CAREFUL TO MANAGE TIME - TIME DOES NOT MANAGE YOU! Because we blink and the year has gone.

UNIT 12

SILVER SURFERS, WOMEN WARRIORS

I have attended a women-only boot camp. I was so eager to attend and trained hard for this. It was on my list of the things to achieve in 2014.

The month before, I had yet again forgiven my mother for not supporting me over a vicious sexual attack in 2013. It has taken me a year to come to terms with her behaviour and lack of support. I only decided to forgive AGAIN due to my faith. I was in Rome during Christmas of 2013 and visited the Vatican twice, where I received a blessing from the Pope. In June 2014 I was then a Guest Key Note Speaker, elevated for the World Leadership Conference through www.g-case.com. I visited the Duomo in Milan one Sunday and sat in the square – paid 10 euros for a coffee – rip off but delightful and watched a Military Service and attended church there. I then decided it was time to forgive and more forward.

I returned from Italy and on that Saturday attended my local church fete. I was speaking to the vicar and my mother as if by fate, was at his side. She asked me if I had time for a coffee. I went along. That day I was going to book my summer holiday to Sorrento and so was she. She said, "Can we go together?" I was reluctant, as it was moving too quickly and I was having a panic attack at the thought of it. Again, fate had it that as we went into our local travel agent's, a cancellation of one of our favourite hotels came up at a ridiculous price. So what do you think we did? Yes, we took it.

Though this calm before another storm was short lived as it always is. .

Whilst at the boot camp, which I had prepared myself for mentally and physically, those bloody self-doubts crept back in like they had since I was young. Even when it was my Primary School Sports Day – wanting to win knowing I could win but my Parents did not attend and in the back of my mind my mother's words of criticism took over – that I was not good enough. So, I came 2nd – when I should have come first. So now here we are again in my 50's and self-doubting myself again because of those little voices in my head. I struggled with this and though in a Run came 12-25 and then on day 2 10/25 and I was the oldest and had not run since school and I was never a long-distance runner but a Sprinter. It was my pride not to finish last. And on day 2 to better my position to beat two of the other young ladies who I shared a dorm with who were half my age but to prove to myself that I could do this. I used my strength of sprinting on the flats and downhill and as I ran I shouted to myself Karen come on you can do this and do this you will?

Why did I allow this to happen to me again, to let my mother's criticism of me take over at this stage? I felt I had let myself down. I had to break that cycle. A friend advised me to jump in a circle and not to let anyone who aimed to harm me to jump in. So I did exactly that.

It's time to STEP UP and STAND OUT, brilliant women.

Here are nine ways you can start to own your brilliance and share it:

1. Decide to take responsibility for you

Take responsibility for or what you want, not what you will settle for.

Make a deal with yourself to be your own supportive friend at every step along the way to where you want to go, because no one else is going to build the life you want you.

The most amazing people will show up to help you on along the way, but it's your responsibility to change and grow.

2. Imagine it

What is the dream you don't allow yourself to even consider because it seems too unrealistic, frivolous, or insane?

What is the career that seems so incredible you think it's almost criminal to have it?

Start envisioning it, because that's the first step to having it.

3. Take more risks

Start doing things that make you feel uncomfortable and get the adrenalin flowing.

Your fears will start to surface. That's normal. Be aware of what beliefs are limiting you because that's the first step to changing them.

4. Stop wanting to be liked

If you take risks, sometimes you'll get a standing ovation and sometimes, people will throw rotten fruit.

Get used to wins and losses, praise and criticism, getting a callback and being ignored.

Work on letting go of needing to be liked and needing to be universally known as "a nice person."

5. Question the voice that says, "I'm not ready yet"

Because you are so brilliant and have such high standards, you notice every part of your idea that is not yet perfect.

While you are waiting to be ready—gathering more experience, sitting on your ideas—others (usually men) are being recognised as experts, getting promoted and seeing their ideas come to fruition.

They are no more ready than you and often less so. Step up and start playing full out.

6. Don't wait for someone to put the tiara on your head

Don't wait to be noticed, praised, or validated.

Don't wait for someone to give you permission to lead.

Don't wait for someone to invite you to share your voice.

No one is going to discover you; you must actively do things to get yourself noticed.

7. Ask for the feedback you want

Most brilliant women are humble and regularly seek feedback on how they are doing.

Be aware that most people don't know how to give you the feedback you need to improve.

Learn to ask for the type of feedback that will help you grow and develop.

Then test and evaluate it based on where you want to go, rather than following it wholesale.

8. Celebrate your successes

If you start doing the things that make you feel uncomfortable, doing what you don't quite feel ready to do, you are going to be stretching your comfort zone, growing and developing.

You should acknowledge the steps you've taken and celebrate your success.

9. Let other women know they are brilliant

Let them know what kind of brilliance you see and why it's so special.

Let them know that you are ready and encourage them to STEP UP and STAND OUT too!

It is so important for us women to support other women, not only in business but also in life. I would not have gotten through my ordeal if it had not been for my BFF Sheila and other true friends who are also my business partners: Lucy, Stephanie and Kristine. Thank you and I respect and love you. x

MIDLIFE CRISIS

This statement normally conjures up images of in men running off with much younger women or buying expensive fast sports cars or for women it is maybe the woman hangs out with a younger crowd or man and even relives her youth. I relive my youth dancing the night away with my girlfriends at the Soul Night in Chester every quarter dancing to some old tunes and with us girls dancing the same old dance moves. But we are not having a 'mid life crisis' we are just having fun as we did then without any worries or inhibitions but now we have those worries and just for one night only we throw the inhibitions out of the window and boy does it feel good....

Three years ago, Christina Vuleta had just quit her job to start her own consulting firm and discovered an energy and thirst for reinvention among the over-forty crowd. Christina wanted to create a 40 Over 40 list as an antidote to all the 30 Under 30 lists, a list that would highlight the significant achievements and momentum of women over forty. She and I became acquainted through The Li.st, a community of women involved in technology, media and entrepreneurship. When she told me about her idea, I'll confess I was hoping to be an honoured over-forty—but when she invited me to create the 40 Over 40 list, it was too exciting to pass up. As both of us looked around, we didn't see women opting out and chucking their dreams; we saw women, including ourselves, getting scrappy and creating new dreams.

Two years and thousands of nominations later, we are in awe of the women who earned their spot on this list—some of whom you've heard of, many of whom you haven't. What they all have in common is that they have more ahead of them than behind them. We are thrilled at the opportunity to inspire these forty-plus individuals to persist despite age stereotypes whilst motivating women in their twenties and thirties in seeing new possibilities by placing a spotlight on the forty-plus set's achievements.

Contrary to popular opinion, the future does not belong only to the young. It is in all our hands to create it. We aren't out to out-do the 30 Under 30 and 40 Under 40 movers and shakers; we just think it's time to recognise the "over" half, who are also transforming the world. This year's over forty honouree's range in age from their forties to their seventies.

Take that, midlife crisis!

We worked with a panel of advisors and judges, which

included many of last year's honouree's as well as an external panel from the tech, entrepreneurial, media and corporate world. Each judge reviewed the candidates based on a set of criteria that places value not only accomplishments but also forward movement and impact:

- Impact: Are they creating growth or making in impact in their field of work, community and beyond?
- Role Model: Is this person a positive role model through mentoring, leading by example, innovating around work/ life issues, building diverse communities, or promoting women for leadership. whether in business or board rooms?
- Momentum: Does this person have more in front of them than behind them? Are they taking on new challenges and harnessing the power of their experiences?

These Women Warriors are not having a midlife crisis: Women that Mentor.

Karen Carter, one of the highest-ranking women at the Dow Chemical Company. In 2013, she was the only woman with a P/L on the global leadership team for Dow's $15 billion packaging and plastics business. Per the woman who nominated her, "Karen has been a role model and mentor to many females and minority employees. She has been my mentor for ten years."

The list includes entrepreneurs such as **Erin McKean**, a lexicographer (dictionary editor) by training who made her way to Silicon Valley by way of a 2007 TED talk that described how the English language is far too big for any paper dictionary to hold. A wife, mother and author who has written about fashion, Erin is now the founder of Reverb Technologies, a content discovery reader.

Mauria Finley, founder of the rapidly growing start-up Citrus Lane, brought the subscription business model to the parenting/ baby market, delivering curated "best of" products suited to a child's developmental stage and product preferences to new parents overwhelmed by choices.

There are activists, philanthropists and musicians. **Farah Mohamed** is the founder and CEO of G(girls)20, who works to change how prime ministers and presidents think by convening girls from throughout the world to speak with world leaders.

As Director of the Vodafone Americas Foundation, **June Sugiyama** is the mastermind behind the Vodafone Wireless Innovation Project that seeks to identify and fund the best innovations using wireless-related technology to address critical social issues around the world.

Singer/songwriter **Hilary Weeks's** most recent album charted in the Top 10 Contemporary Christian Charts. After learning that the average person thinks 300 negative thoughts per day, she launched billionclicks.org to promote positive thinking.

And there are women applying their change-making passion to a completely new area, such as **Sallie Krawcheck**, once known as the "most powerful woman on Wall Street" with former executive roles at Bank of America and Citigroup. Krawcheck recently acquired 85 Broads, a women's networking organisation now known as Ellevate and has launched the Pax Ellevate Global Women's Index Fund, the first and only mutual fund in the United States that focuses on investing in companies that are global leaders in advancing women.

The full list of winners can be found at **40 Women to Watch over 40.**

Over the past two years, the list has quickly found support across generations and genders. A fair number of nominations were made by men. And we were delighted to see both young and women were eager to be involved. Twenty-somethings **Molly Ford**, a blogger and digital marketer and **Pooja Parthasarathy**, a financial analyst, both joined the organising committee to gain access to more varied mentors in their own lives and to champion women in all stages of their careers. And fifty-something **Patti Finn Bumgardner** came on board to get inspiration to restart her own career after ramping off as a mum.

Similarly, the external judging panel included a high-calibre, diverse mix of both men and women:

- **Adam Grant:** Wharton professor, author, NY Times Best-seller *Give & Take*
- **Binta Niambi Brown:** Lawyer, start-up advisor, human rights advocate, Davos Young Global Leader
- **Courtney Boyd-Myers:** Founder, audience.io
- **John Eczema:** NY Times Bestseller *The Athena Doctrine, Social Strategist*
- **Justin Stanwix:** Director, Friends of eBay
- **Vanu Bose:** CEO/Founder of Vanu, Inc.

Life begins at fifty for SME high-fliers! It is now a fact that 54 percent of all entrepreneurs in 2013 were over fifty, and only 2 percent were under twenty-five!

Business Money: New research shows that many of the owner-managers of the UK's fastest growing businesses are fifty years old and older, shattering media perceptions of young entrepreneurs being the chief engineers of SME success stories. This research was conducted by the Cranfield School of Business UK, led by Professor Andrea Burke. Through our alternative-funding non-banking options through www.gateway2enterprie.co.uk, we have found that this age group prefers to release monies from their pensions to set up businesses.

So, if you now want the life you deserve and have a business idea, we are happy to fund it through a Personal with FREE Mentoring with one of our Business Advisors. If you have an idea that has been sitting there gathering dust and you don't need investment and now that you are free to live your life and your dreams – need an alternative income, maybe invest in a Lifestyle Business then join us as part of our SSEC CLUB, where we will support you with our SSEC PACKAGE through www.gateway2enterprise.co.uk. We are working with over 40 different Funding organisations within the UK.

The level of self-employment in the fifty-plus age group is about one in five, considerably higher than levels across all ages.

Reasons for this upsurge in "Silver Surfers Entrepreneurs," as they have been dubbed by the media, include:

- earlier retirement or enforced redundancy,
- low-interest rates,
- the abandonment of the statutory retirement age,
- the demise of final-salary pensions,
- and a fashionable desire to reinvent yourself in another form, preferably one that supplements your state pension.

BUSINESS SUCCESS

This growing army of entrepreneurs could potentially add billions to the UK economy in the coming years if current predictions are correct.

Years of collected experience and expertise means that this group of start-up entrepreneurs is more likely to succeed, with over 70 percent lasting more than five years, compared with 28 percent of younger entrepreneurs.

With the over-fifty-fives due to account for a third of the UK's population by 2025, older workers are well placed to take advantage of this fast-growing marketplace through shared experience and understanding.

So, what kind of businesses are we talking about? They tend to be small-scale, quite often home-based and modestly financed, but their natures range hugely, from genealogy to speciality catering to self-care for women experiencing menopause.

Per Hilary Farnworth, who runs start-up courses for the over-fifties at the Metropolitan University, women prefer to be sole traders, whereas men generally prefer to go into partnership with other like-minded men.

I am aware that in the USA they have the www.sba.gov and www.encore.org to support this growing client group; the SBA particularly is supportive of women in business. In the UK, we do have PRIME, which is part of the Princes' Trust and of course in the UK, as in the USA, there are franchises designed for this market.

Dr Penelope Keough is one of my dearest colleagues and friend – www-g-casa.com

Karen Melanie Gould and I, Dr Penelope Keough, met as literary women warriors. We found we had a commonality in reaching other women who had struggled with reaching for the "glass ceiling" and at times, not always able to penetrate.

Karen and I met at Chinese American Scholars conference in Milan, Italy. What struck me first about her was her outgoing personality and the willingness to know everyone in the room by shaking hands!

I had just read the book, Mindset, by Carol Dweck and Karen had just written a book about the mindset for the "Happy Entrepreneur".

We had immediate chemistry! In sharing the day together, we discovered hardships life had dealt us which only has made us stronger and ready to face any challenge that comes along.

My life is richer for our relationship and each new meeting together brings with it fresh ideas to tackle the next entrepreneurial adventure!

Penny and I are Women Warriors that will remain friends throughout time and support each other. Penny stays with me in the UK and for Penny's big birthday coming up in January 2017 we are off to Spain to share this moment in Penny's life. I am so blessed to have genuine friends who reach out to me from across the pond. Love you Penny x

UNIT 13

WOMEN WARRIORS NEVER GIVE UP

I HAD JUST SURVIVED a week from hell with staffing and technical issues on my finance comparison site. On Friday night I got a frantic call from one of our partners, shouting abuse down the phone to me to get my "fu**king details off your site" before we all get banned by the FCA. I nearly turned to drink but did not and instead thought about solutions for the problems to start fresh Monday morning. I was about to give into a VC offer and sell it off under-priced, as I had had enough! Then I read an article by this lady about being in the driver's seat:

NAOMI SIMPSON - RED BALLOONS

Some of the best advice I was given was simply: **"You are in control of your own life. Get in the driver's seat, take the wheel and steer."**

The famous quote from Winston Churchill resonates with me and whilst he was talking about wartime, the words remain powerful:

Never give in. Never give in. Never, never, never,
never—in nothing, great or small, large or petty—
never give in, except to convictions of honour and good

sense. Never yield to force. Never yield to the apparently overwhelming might of the enemy."

- Winston S. Churchill

The best advice comes from within. Trust and have faith in yourself. Always go with your gut feeling or your sixth sense.

UNIT 14

DISPELLING THE "MYTH" OF THE GLASS CEILING

THIS TERM IS USED TO describe an invisible "barrier" that prevents advancement in someone's career—in this instance, women.

Per a Report ILM 2012, most women aspiring to senior management positions believe the glass ceiling to career progression still exists.

The survey of 3,000 members of the Institute of Leadership and Management (ILM) found 73 percent of female respondents felt barriers still existed for women seeking senior management and board-level positions in the UK. In contrast, just 38 percent of men believed there is a glass ceiling.

But then this glass ceiling is lifting as Women Warriors take the lead in business. The findings, which came from an even sample of men and women with an average age of 43, also revealed that 24 percent of women under 30 expected to start their own businesses within ten years, compared with 20 percent of men!

Penny de Valk, the institute's chief executive, said the pressure on many women to combine childcare with career aspirations was "part of the cocktail." If large organisations wanted to nurture the talent of their best female employees, they needed to start challenging some of the unwritten rules of what senior management roles looked like.

"It's not that women are risk-averse; younger women, in particular, are incredibly ambitious around entrepreneurial activity. Yet we can see that a promotion path within a large organisation is almost seen as riskier for them, on a personal basis, than going out and setting up their own venture," she said.

Regardless of gender and any barriers, whether obvious or not, leaders are born, not made, in my opinion—and great leaders don't normally make great managers.

Of late in the UK and on social media there are many debates on this subject and now many boards in the UK have been set up to tackle this issue of gender discrimination. I have been asked to speak at the Women's Power Conference Liverpool March 2015, having just been a speaker at the Liverpool Women in Business Conference Feb 2015. I am very cautious of having myself stereotyped into championing this "Glass Ceiling," as I find it a myth.

I have held senior corporate positions in the UK and USA. Though I will agree that it is easy for you to secure and hang onto them when you are under 35 and that the older you get the harder it is to compete with your male 30-something colleagues, it is not because you don't have the energy—it is because they see you as more of a threat and will form a male-bonded group to undermine you. Beware these naïve young males, but also beware the woman who convinces you of her "sisterhood," support, and admiration, when in fact, her jealousy/envy is hidden well.

I have had many women on my ILM Programs for Leadership and Management Level 5/7 over the last ten years who have been through the corporate ladder on an international level and been chewed up and spat out—and it all seemed to happen when they hit a certain age: 35-plus.

Unfortunately, I do agree that as men get older in corporate business, they are revered and put on a pedestal for their maturity, hence experience. But for women, it is a different matter—you must earn it and then demonstrate it and then endorse it.

For those women on my programs I will open two case studies:

Sharon – Barrister – Sharon was finding it harder to juggle her level of work with travel and raising a family. So, Sharon came to a sensible decision that she would evaluate her skills and re-train. Sharon trained as a coach/mentor and now runs a very successful women's organisation in Manchester UK (www.lifecolourcoach.com), running workshops with women on how to become confident and proactive to take control of your own destiny. I am very proud that I mentored Sharon.

Catherine – Catherine had a very successful corporate career in marketing on an international platform. When Catherine first came to me in 2012, she was completely "broken" and so lost that she was not aware of where she was going in her career. Catherine went through my programs and we supported her to start her own business in marketing; then I asked her to run my business club, which she did with a dedicated professionalism. Catherine came to work for me in 2014 as a business mentor and that seemed to go well. From the quality of her work and the dedication of her time, there was nothing but praise. But underneath, Catherine had other issues. I feel that her industry did not chew her up when she hit 40, but that she had already acquired a drinking habit that affected her judgement, as this behaviour then manifested itself in her role with me. Also, I started to observe Catherine with our male members of staff and noted her praising them all the time; then she started to undermine me to include them. Eventually, Catherine's behaviour towards me (which my HR manager put down to that "green-eyed monster") became abusive. I had to let Catherine go at the end of 2014 with regret, but there was no other choice.

UNIT 15

WHAT TYPE OF WOMAN WARRIOR ARE YOU?

I AM A WOMAN WHO loves and adore women and does not put men on a pedestal. I believe that we are equal and perhaps more capable of succeeding; they call it in industry "Raising the Glass Ceiling." Unfortunately, some women only want to bring women down and hate to see women succeed. They are hard to spot sometimes, as they pretend to like you and say that they are there for you; however, having found out the hard way, sometimes they will cut you at the knees. SO BE AWARE! If you find them within your organisation, they must be weeded out and removed.

Surround yourself with like-minded women who will encourage, inspire and motivate you by supporting you to succeed. I am one of those ladies—are you?

INSPIRATION – These Women Warriors come in many forms, for many reasons and at different chapters in your life. My grandmother was there for me growing up. Then at school, I had two English teachers, Mrs Ford and Miss Wright and several PE instructors who encouraged me in my English (whether it was poetry or writing or public speaking) and then with my sports (from dancing and network to swimming). Then in the last ten years, since I have regained my confidence in business again, I am surrounded by incredible Women Warriors in business and in life.

MOTHER – Rosemary is an incredible, beautiful lady who is highly intelligent and has beaten the big C and is now living life to the full. My mother and I will never be best friends, but she is still an incredible force to be reckoned with.

WHAT TYPE OF WOMAN WARRIOR, IF AT ALL A WOMAN WARRIOR?

If you are a mother – sister – grandmother – sister-in-law – aunt or something similar, and if you have nurtured another female within your family or circle of friends to live fulfilled and happy lives, then you can wear this badge with honour!

An example from my personal journey in life would be my grandmother, Isabella, who always believed in me and never doubted my capabilities nor my talent, who nurtured and encouraged me to do well, whether it was through dance, sport, acting, teaching, or even relationships. I loved her dearly.

If you are a true friend to other women—not because you feel you should fit into a certain social circle or impress a peer group—and if you have supported a female friend through the difficult times: when they have lost a loved one, moved house, gone through a divorce/separation, or lost their job, then you cannot just wear this badge with honour, but you can give it a shine!

My example for this group would be one of my BBFs, Sheila, who started out with me on one of our Career Management Programs over seven years ago in Warrington on my JOB/Work Club for Executives. Sheila became and still is one of my mentors on this program. Sheila had a very successful career in HR Corporate and in the Intelligence Service in the RAF and then came to us having been through a period of long-term illness and looking for a real life balance of change in her life. Sheila then became and still is one of my BFFs and without her support and strength in 2013, when I was severely attacked and raped whilst on holiday in Italy, I would not be here today. Supporting other women to overcome any barrier to living a happy and fulfilled life, is most enjoyable for me, as we deserve it girls.

If you are or have been a mentor, coach, or business associate and if within your organisation or business you have used your skills to enable other women to grow, then you too can wear this badge with honour!

I have mentored thousands of women over the last ten years through my many programs, some of which are Women-Only programs in employment and business. I cannot single out any one of them,

PROFILE OF EMILY MORTON – MENTEE

I first came to meet Emily at UCLAN Preston, when she joined one of my Rockstar Workshops in the summer of 2013. First impressions are not always a good guideline, as when I first met Emily, she was and still is on crutches and in pain just walking around to everyday events. Emily did not at first come across to me as very confident and indeed her appearance at that time led me to believe that she was suffering some form of depression. Emily joined the group and then, when it was her turn to introduce herself, I was blown away with her knowledge, skills and expertise in the record industry. Emily certainly does not present herself as someone who has this immense knowledge of this industry and is not the stereotype of this industry, but boy, she owns it. I have been mentoring Emily since then, to set up her various record management companies and against all the odds, due to her ill health, she has never ceased to amaze me and I would have to say she is one of the hardest, most conscientious Women Warrior mentees that I have ever had the pleasure and honour to mentor. After a painful operation in the summer of 2015 and after her beloved dog died, I am pleased to know that Emily is re-joining me on my business club for September 2015 and has also joined a local charity, which I support as a volunteer in events.

If you are in a position of power within politics, business, the church, or within another hierarchy and if you have used your power to instrument change for women, then you too can wear this badge with honour.

Emily is still following her dreams but has had some setbacks within her personal life with having to have several operations affecting her walking and some counselling to deal with some personal childhood issues. Emily is looking into fostering again.

Emily is a strong young woman although childhood experiences that are unpleasant don't go away and can only become a bigger problem as we get older.

UNIT 16

EMPOWERING WOMEN

MEANING AND MEAN IT – to give some the control to make decisions that shape their lives and to do this they must act.

I want to look across the pond, firstly the first black female Attorney General in the USA: Loretta Lynch.

As the first African American woman in U.S. history to be sworn in as Attorney General, Loretta Lynch's appointment marks an important milestone for minority women in leadership roles.

Currently, black women make up only 1 percent of U.S. corporate officers, even though 75 percent of corporate executives now believe having minorities in senior level positions fosters innovation and better serves a diverse customer base. While the appointment of Lynch as Attorney General took longer than the last seven attorney generals combined, it is a win for women, a win for racial minorities and a win for every citizen who believes that diversity is crucial to effective leadership, sound governance and genuine equality.

Let's start with gender. A recent report by the Pew Research Centre shows that Americans feel more positive about women than men in both politics and management. Given the low popularity ratings of government, this should bring some hope to generating results in the Justice Department.

While most Americans (over 60 percent) believe, gender has no bearing on a person's ability to be honest and ethical, those who do perceive a difference believe women are better at being honest and ethical than men. In fact, the number of those who feel women have the edge is ten times greater than those who believe that men do. Similar advantages are perceived when focusing on who is better at improving U.S. quality of life (five to one in favour of women) and collaborating across multiple interests and working out compromises (four to one in favour of women). Not only that, a June 2011 *Harvard Business Review* study found that a team›s overall intelligence is determined more by the gender of its members than by their individual IQ's and that the inclusion of women raises the performance of the team.

Surveys such as these support more optimistic expectations for the leadership of the U.S. Justice Department. Since women's leadership tends to promote "getting along" versus the male-driven "getting ahead" approach, we ought to see some radical changes in the Justice Department—more cooperation, less gridlock, better outcomes.

Next, diversity-based research has shown that racially diverse leadership is associated with better outcomes. This can be largely attributed to the fact that racially diverse candidates have a heightened sensitivity to integrating the needs of disparate constituents.

Given the current racial unrest in the country—New York, Florida, Missouri and most recently in Baltimore, Maryland—one would hope that having a black Attorney General will help ease the malcontent and restore calm to the wave of violence that has swept across the U.S. in recent months. If President Obama is correct, this isn't a race issue—it is a police brutality issue and a black female Attorney General will almost certainly bring a new perspective and different approach to addressing this problem.

I will want to see what Loretta can bring to the table and what she will do not only for black women but for women and humanity in general by leading in the USA for the rest of the world to follow.

Secondly, I wanted to look at Hilary Clinton.

Hillary Clinton has served as Secretary of State, a senator from New York, First Lady of the United States, First Lady of Arkansas, a practicing lawyer and law professor, activist and volunteer, but the first things her friends and family will tell you is that she's never forgotten where she came from or who she's been fighting for throughout her life.

Hillary's mother, Dorothy, had a tough childhood. She was abandoned by her parents as a young child and shipped off to live with relatives who didn't want her. By age of fourteen, Dorothy knew the only way she'd get by was to support herself and she started working as a housekeeper and babysitter while she went through high school. Her mother's experience sparked in Hillary a lifelong commitment to championing the needs of children.

Her own childhood was very different. Her parents built a stable middle-class life. Hillary attended public schools and was a Brownie and a Girl Scout. She played in a girls' softball league. She was brought up as a Methodist and her mum taught Sunday school. Her youth minister took Hillary to see Martin Luther King, Jr. speak in Chicago and helped her develop a life-long passion for social justice.

Hillary graduated from Wellesley College and then went to Yale Law School, where she was one of just twenty-seven women in her graduating class. Hillary met her husband Bill at Law school.

After Law school, Hillary chose not to go to a big New York or Washington law firm. Instead, she went to work for the Children's Defence Fund, going door to door in New Bedford, Massachusetts, gathering stories about the lack of schooling for children with disabilities, which contributed to the passage of historic legislation to require their education.

It's this commitment to public service and fighting for others—especially children and families—that she's carried all her life.

After serving as a lawyer for the congressional committee investigating President Nixon, she moved to Arkansas, where she taught law and ran legal clinics representing poor people. She co-founded Arkansas Advocates for Children and Families, one of the state's first child advocacy groups. And on October 11, 1975, she married Bill in a small ceremony in Fayetteville, Arkansas. As First Lady of Arkansas, she was a forceful champion for improving educational standards and health care access. And she and Bill started their own family when their daughter, Chelsea, was born in 1980.

Bill was first elected president in 1992 and re-elected in 1996. As First Lady, Hillary tenaciously led the fight to reform the USA health care system so that all families could have access to the care they needed at affordable prices. When the insurance companies and other special interests defeated that effort, Hillary didn't give up. She worked with Republicans and Democrats to help create the successful Children's Health Insurance Program, which provides health coverage to more than 8 million children and has helped cut the uninsured rate for children in half.

In 1995, despite being told by some officials not to go, Hillary led the U.S. delegation to Beijing to attend the UN Fourth World Conference on Women and gave a ground-breaking speech, declaring that "human rights are women's rights and women's rights are human rights once and for all"—inspiring women worldwide and helping to galvanize a global movement for women's rights and opportunities.

In 2000, Hillary was elected to the U.S. Senate, becoming the first woman senator from New York. After the terrorist attacks of September 11, 2001, Hillary pushed the Bush Administration to secure $20 billion to rebuild New York and fought to provide health care for first responders, who were contaminated at Ground Zero. She repeatedly worked across the aisle to get things done, including working alongside Republicans to expand TRICARE so that members of the Reserves and National Guard and their families could get better access to health care.

When Congress wouldn't do enough for rural areas and small towns, Hillary didn't back down. She launched an innovative partnership in New York with eBay and local colleges to provide small businesses with tech support, microloans and training programs to sell their goods online. She helped expand broadband to remote areas of the state. And she launched Farm-to-Fork, to help New York farmers and producers sell their products to New York's restaurants, schools, colleges and universities.

In 2008, Hillary ran for president. When she came up short, she told her supporters, "Although we could shatter that highest, hardest glass ceiling this time, thanks to you, it's got about 18 million cracks in it."

And when President Obama asked Hillary to serve as his

secretary of state, she put aside their hard-fought campaign and answered the call to public service once again. After eight years of Bush foreign policy, Hillary was instrumental in starting to restore America's standing in the world. Even former Republican Secretary of State Henry Kissinger said she "ran the State Department in the most effective way that I've ever seen."

In 2014, Hillary took on a new role—grandmother to Charlotte Clinton Mezvinsky—and she couldn't be prouder or happier. Hilary failed again in 2016 to become the first female President but I don't think that is the last we have heard from her.

Now I will look at two women that I greatly admire in the UK who have achieved greatness for women in politics.

Firstly, I would like to look at **Betty Boothroyd,** the British Politician.

The enormous respect and affection of the British public for Betty Boothroyd has its roots in a strong belief in what she stands for: fair play, an unshakeable sense of honour and a passionate belief in the sovereignty of Parliament. Her convictions, she has said, are set in "Yorkshire granite." Born into a working-class family in Dewsbury in 1929, there was little money, but Betty grew up in a home that radiated love and warmth. Betty was popular and a talented dancer who eventually went on to become one of the celebrated Tiller Girls—the full story of which she tells here for the first time. But by the age of twenty-five, Betty's dreams of taking the West End by storm had crashed—and her father's ambition of seeing her settled with a nice, safe job had been abandoned. Undaunted, she won a national speaking award, stood for election to the local council and became a full-time worker for the Labour Party. Nothing would ever part Betty

Boothroyd from politics again. In 1953 Betty began work at the House of Commons for Barbara Castle and Geoffrey de Freitas.

She speaks candidly about the devastation of losing two by-elections and the time she spent in America campaigning for JFK. Back in Britain, Betty landed a top job with millionaire Labour Minister Lord Harry Walston and the Yorkshire girl became part of the inner circle of the socialist elite, which included Hugh Gaitskell and Roy Jenkins. She describes the elation she felt on becoming an MP at last in 1973, the huge debt she owes her mother for her support and the full story behind her role in the struggle to save the Labour Party from the hard left. Betty Boothroyd's long political career reached its apogee in 1992 when she was appointed the first woman Speaker of the House of Commons with overwhelming support from both sides of the House. Her term of office coincided with John Major's attempts to defend his slim majority. Detailing many of the true stories behind the headlines, she writes of the sleaze scandals that beset the Major government, her feelings when Labour won their landslide election in 1997 and her strongly held views on the role of Parliament.

Finally, she tells why she decided to retire, her plans and—in retrospect—what she feels about her decision to put public service above marriage.

Of course, we could not discuss British history in politics without mentioning the "Iron Lady" herself—**Maggie Thatcher**.

Margaret Thatcher has always been one of my heroines of the modern age, a "Woman Warrior."

My mother will never forgive her for the Falklands War in 1982, where my brother served on a supply ship that was bombed by the Argentine Air Force. The Bluff Cove Air Attacks occurred 8 June 1982, during the Falklands War. British troop transport ships were bombed by the Argentine Air Force (FAA) whilst unloading, with significant damage and casualties. My brother still has nightmares to this day of trying to rescue burning bodies, though he has never spoken about it. He then went on to have epileptic fits, was unable to play rugby and had to change his job many times. He also ended up having a treble heart bypass at the age of fifty and must watch his weight—but don't we all?

I loved this period working in London Hedonistic and for a woman, it was the wild 80s followed by the naughty 90s. I don't think that Mrs Thatcher was a feminist at all and did not do much directly for women's rights. Mrs Thatcher had three terms as PM, so the country must have felt she did a pretty good job, especially in comparison to the "wimps" we have today.

My grandmother used to froth at the mouth when she came on the TV and so did my grandmother, or she did to get approval from my grandfather who was selfish pig of a man, self-centred and vain and an absent father and husband as he was too busy chasing young women and spending his money on them. My grandmother idolised him and never questioned anything he did or said. He had contempt for her and would ridicule her in front of other people; he was a weak man. I quickly learnt how to get my own way with him, as I was a lot cleverer than most of his female children so used to flatter him endlessly and this worked—plus he could boast about me, as I was always winning something at school from Sports to Poetry to Public Speaking.

Born on 13th October 1925, in Grantham, England, Margaret Thatcher became Britain's Conservative Party leader and in 1979 was elected prime minister, the first woman to hold the position. During her three terms, she cut social welfare programs, reduced trade union power and privatised certain industries. Thatcher resigned in 1991 due to unpopular policy and power struggles in her party. She died on April 8, 2013, at age 87.

Margaret Thatcher: A young Margaret Roberts (right) stands for a portrait with her parents and sister, Muriel. Margaret later changed her last name after marrying British businessman Denis Thatcher in 1951.

Margaret Thatcher read her Bachelor of Science degree in chemistry from Oxford in 1947. During her first run for political office in 1950, she supported herself by working as a research chemist.

Nicknamed the "Iron Lady," Thatcher served as the prime minister of England from 1979 to 1990. The daughter of a local businessman, she was educated at a local grammar school, Grantham Girls' High School. Her family operated a grocery store and they all lived in an apartment above the store. In her early years, Thatcher was introduced to conservative politics by her father, who was a member of the town's council.

A good student, Thatcher was accepted to Oxford University, where she studied chemistry at Somerville College. One of her instructors was the Dorothy Hodgkin, a Nobel-Prize-winning scientist. Politically active in her youth, Thatcher served as president of the Conservative Association at the university. She earned a degree in chemistry in 1947 and went on to work as a research chemist in Colchester. Later, she worked as a research chemist in Dartford.

EARLY FORAY INTO POLITICS

Two years after graduating from college, Thatcher made her first bid for public office. She ran as the conservative candidate for a Dartford parliamentary seat in the 1950 elections. Thatcher knew from the start that it would be nearly impossible to win the position away from the liberal Labour Party. Still, she earned the respect of her political party peers with her speeches. Defeated, Thatcher remained undaunted, trying again the following year, but once more her efforts were unsuccessful. Two months after her loss, she married Denis Thatcher.

In 1952, Thatcher put politics aside for a time to study law. She and her husband welcomed twins, Carol and Mark, the next year. After completing her training, Thatcher qualified as a barrister in 1953. But she didn't stay away from the political arena for too long. Thatcher won a seat in the House of Commons in 1959, representing Finchley.

Clearly a woman on the rise, Thatcher was appointed parliamentary Undersecretary for Pensions and National Insurance in 1961. When the Labour Party assumed control of the government, she became a member of what is called the Shadow Cabinet, a group of political leaders who would hold Cabinet-level posts if their party was in power.

BRITAIN'S FIRST FEMALE PREMIER

When Conservatives returned to office in June 1970, Thatcher was appointed Secretary of State for Education and Science and dubbed "Thatcher, milk snatcher" after her abolition of the universal free school milk scheme. She found her position frustrating, not because of all the bad press around her actions, but because she had difficulty getting Prime Minister Edward Heath to listen to her ideas. Seemingly disenchanted on the future of women in politics, Thatcher was quoted as saying, "I don't think there will be a woman prime minister in my lifetime" during a 1973 television appearance.

Thatcher soon proved herself wrong. While the Conservative Party lost power in 1974, Thatcher became a dominant force in her political party. She was elected leader of the Conservative Party in 1975, beating out Heath for the position. With this victory, Thatcher became the first woman to serve as the opposition leader in the House of Commons. England was in a time of economic and political turmoil, with the government nearly bankrupt, unemployment on the rise and conflicts with labour unions. This instability helped return Conservatives to power in 1979. As party leader, Thatcher made history in May 1979, when she was appointed Britain's first female prime minister.

Thatcher faced a military challenge during her first term. In April 1982, Argentina invaded the Falkland Islands. This British territory had long been a source of conflict between the two nations, as the islands are located off the coast of Argentina. Taking swift action, Thatcher sent British troops to the territory to retake the islands in what became known as the Falklands War. Argentina surrendered in June 1982.

RESIGNATION

Returning for a third term in 1987, Thatcher sought to implement a standard educational curriculum across the nation and make changes to the country's socialised medical system. However, she lost a lot of support due to her efforts to implement a fixed rate local tax—labelled a poll tax by many, since she sought to disenfranchise those who did not pay it. Hugely unpopular, this policy led to public protests and caused dissension within her party.

Thatcher initially pressed on for the party leadership in 1990 but eventually yielded to pressure from party members and announced her intentions to resign on November 22, 1990. In a statement, she said:

Having consulted widely among colleagues, I have concluded that the unity of the Party and the prospects of victory in a General Election would be better served if I stood down to enable Cabinet colleagues to enter the ballot for the leadership. I should like to thank all those in Cabinet and outside who have given me such dedicated support.

On November 28, 1990, Thatcher departed from 10 Downing Street, the prime minister's official residence, for the last time.

Maggie Thatcher sadly passed away in 2010 and in my view, she was one of the greatest female leaders of all time. Maggie made the 80's 90's rock for me in business and in my personal life and opened up so many opportunities. From Education to career choice to owning your own home and to standing up and being counted!

For me, I grew up in London and had my first job and flatshare in London; it seemed normal to have a woman leading our country and it gave me tremendous confidence in my job, my wellbeing – with men and more. I was living the high life in London and loving every minute of it; "Thatcherism" endorsed in us to "live life to the full," and I went along with it with all the other women at that time in business, politics, music and more. Maggie inspired me to make the big changes in my life, which I did—I left the UK to find myself and my future, first in Europe and then the USA.

The new 'Woman Warrior' a ground-breaking heroine – the new type of Boudicca PM Theresa May 2016

The new Thatcher and the one who has taken on Brexit. Theresa May in endorsed in my first book in 2010 'GET BRITAIN WORKING' when she was the Shadow Secretary of State and Work and Pensions. This was part of the Conservatives' www.getbritainworking.com campaign of which I wrote the Job Club/ Work Programs and Business Club and ran these programs in Warrington for 9 years until Dec 2015. Supporting over 500 into employment over 250 new businesses and the growth of a further 150. These programs were sc successful because of the 'A Team' of Mentors whose passion and commitment were in endless supply. I sadly miss these programs, although great to have my Saturdays back, I think of all those lives we changed and impacted on and not just through work and business but in achieving life balance and quality of life and being happy.

Oxford University 2015 have their first Woman Vice Chancellor!

LOUISE RICHARDSON – TERRORISM EXPERT

Louise Mary Richardson FRSE (born 8 June 1958 in Tramore, County Waterford, Ireland) is an Irish political scientist whose specialist field is the study of terrorism. Currently the Principal and Vice-Chancellor of the University of St. Andrews, she was formerly employed at Harvard University, where she served as Executive Dean of the Radcliffe Institute for Advanced Study. On 28 May 2015, the University of Oxford announced that she had been nominated as the next Vice-Chancellor, subject to approval, to take up the post on 1 January 2016. The nomination was approved on 25 June 2015.

UNIT 17

REFLECTION

We have looked back over 2014 - 2016. This reflection is what has prompted some of us to make a promise to ourselves to achieve success in something—even if it is just to win the prize for the best cupcakes at the school fete, join a running club, start a business, go for that promotion at work, or write that book. What have you promised yourself for 2017?

I have set my GOALS for 2017 – try writing down 12 things to achieve this year and put them 1. In Priority and then review them end of the year. I am always happy if I achieve 10/12. I have done so for the past 8 years.

UNIT 18

INFLUENCE

Some of us are lucky enough to have had mothers, grandmothers, or other women close to us to empower us to be successful at something that we know we are good at. My grandmother returned to work to support her family and my mother brought up three children when my father died, whilst holding down a full-time job in the Public Sector. These are early influences, but today, women who shape businesses influence me.

SOCIAL MEDIA MANTRAS

These mantras vow to inspire and motivate you and they are great mantles for celebrities to publicise their wise words—or is it their wise words? Cara Delevingne has stated, "You are not born a winner; you are not born a loser. You are born a chooser." Reese Witherspoon has stated, "Little girls with dreams become women with vision." Beyoncé has stated, "Never let go of that Fiery Sadness called Desire," and so on. The one that stands out to me is from Gilbert Chesterton: "Without the rain—there would be no rainbow." That sums up life to me—we must have a failure to taste success, so there is never a FAILURE because it is part of the journey of learning to find your success through being yourself.

SUPERWOMEN OUT THERE, SLOW DOWN…

I read an interesting article about Arianna Huffington of the Huffington Post and Thrive Workshops and how her sister Agapi Stassinopoulos brought her back from "burnout." Her advice to us is that if you want to achieve—then chill out! I can relate to that, as over the past six years I have been racing through life to catch up to achieve; I felt guilty because I did not achieve what I thought I could have, due to controlling, toxic relationships, from my mother to a partner relationship. I then looked back and before my very eyes it flashed up to me: Karen, you have missed so many opportunities because you were blinkered by being around people who you allowed to damage your confidence and self-worth. Why did I allow these people to influence and control my life like that, to take away from me the success I should have had? I can now identify that in the past I chose bad relationships with men that were not suitable because I lacked self-esteem and did not feel worthy of the love of a more deserving person. My mother's influence on me as a child and young woman had led me to believe that about myself.

So then, in the last six years, having awoken from a bad dream, I have been making up for lost time. I now need to chill and "smell the roses," because I have so much to be thankful for and am blessed by God. I have my health and my looks as I'm reaching a mature age for a woman (over fifty); I work out daily and love to dance and can take myself through a treble Zumba class. I have my integrity in business and three very successful businesses. More importantly, I use my knowledge, skills and experience to support others to achieve in business, having supported over 2,000 businesses in the last three years. I have a loving husband, who is kind and supportive and who stuck by me even when I was a monster to live with. I have a healthy relationship with my mother that must have boundaries set and I make sure that these are observed and respected. I have wonderful, amazing friends like Sheila – Lucy, Lesley, Kristin, Rosemary – Stephanie, Paola – Penny and many more who I know are my true friends, who don't just want me for what I can do for them in business or in their personal life. I have a network of business colleagues, male and female, that I respect and this is returned to me not because I demand it but because I have earned it. I would have liked a more "normal" relationship within my inner family with my sister and brother, but I am working on that and I still love them and wish them happiness.

UNIT 19

MILAN 2014 – LEADERSHIP AND MANAGEMENT CONFERENCE

PAOLA DE VECCHI GALBIATI

MANAGING CONSULTANT DISRUPTIVE INNOVATION AND MEMETICS EXPERT

I MET KAREN AT AN E-Leader Conference 2014 in Milan. She presented her methodology and results achieved through her company and mentoring activities.

She gave us a copy of her new book, *Happy Entrepreneur Mind Set,* and I read this with much interest and curiosity.

I'm a managing consultant and I'm working on a start-up in education, an organisation for SME and P.A. (Public Admin). Of course, this book is for me a practice and useful tool.

I found it very inspiring. Why? Because true stories and true people are told in this book because from its pages a real passion and commitment emerge very clearly.

Applying a mix of scientific approach and humanistic language, Karen observes the enterprise's reality and provides a simple framework to understand and amplify the classic vision of the business.

I read the book very quickly the first time, like a compelling novel, where each chapter tells an important aspect of the protagonist… then you realise that the protagonist can be you.

I re-read this book and I think it will remain a long time on my desk, to consult it often, as I do with an instruction manual or a dictionary, because it allows us to use reason and emotion at the same time on issues and practical problems.

These are times we need to change the way we do things, the way we approach social and business environment, we solve problems always more complex… and this book provides its contribution in changing first the way we see the world and we can collaborate to change us with it.

MILAN E-LEADER CONFERENCE – 3-5 JUNE 2014

By submitting a paper of 10,000 words on this subject, "Happy Entrepreneur Mindset," I was invited to speak at the above conference as a Key Note Speaker. It was such an honour and such a privilege. I met such amazing and dedicated professionals from around the globe through www.g-casa.com, who are truly inspiring and I thank them, as I learnt so much from them. They are certainly making a difference. I sold my advanced copy of this book out there and have been invited to so many awesome events—the conferences and the opportunities are endless. I am looking forward to China in January 2015 and Prague in June 2015. I am also looking forward to meeting up with many of you from this conference and working with you.

I had the pleasure of working with Paola at the Milan Leadership and Management Conference and will repeat this pleasure in Prague June 2015. We have kept in touch and shared our professional moments and supported each other in our commitment to securing change, particularly from where we stand in Leadership and Management and in business.

I wanted to look at Women Warriors around the World for many reasons and felt it was a great place to start with Italy and my dear friend Paola.

PAOLA DE VECCHI GALBIATI

I was lucky to have been born into a family in which the women have never been viewed or stigmatised as secondary to men. Thanks to the behaviours and attitudes of my grandparents and parents, I never considered that there were any difficulties for a woman to express herself and her abilities.

I spent the first ten years of my life playing very much outside. I guess I was a tomboy.

I loved climbing trees, playing football and hitting cans with a sling shot. And while there were my boyfriends who loved to embroider, pick flowers and play with dolls, nobody has ever found anything strange in this.

During the years, I spent in secondary school and in University, I encountered many closed-minded people. Every day I witnessed the concretization of prejudices that I can summarise in this sentence: "These are not things for women."

I saw educated men and women defend a social hierarchy based on a dogma: "There are the men first and after there are women."

It was consuming and it was a conflict between a male-driven society and women's groups seeking to expand landscapes and mindsets.

During my school years, I have really developed into a fighter, who was trying to adapt myself to the world and approach of "businessmen," and the men who controlled most of it.

My path through managerial roles was very rapid: I was a manager at 27 and at the age of 30 I managed the ICT staff of a midsized company and at 37 I was Information System Solutions of a multinational company.

My career accelerated quickly, but it was very tiring. I spent more time convincing my bosses of the value of my ideas than I did executing them.

In the evaluation of my work, I have always received judgments and reviews cloaked in sexism. I had a manager who accused me of being "too motherly with my team," while there were those others who said I was "too assertive with colleagues" and who accused me of being "unfeminine." Then there were others who said I put "too much femininity in doing things." No matter about no discussions about positive results I had achieved. And not one of them ever raised the doubt they had with me that they had exhibited "too much paternalistic" behaviour! With me.

I had reached a high level within this model of hierarchy when I realised that I had no more chances in many contexts—I was running out of advancement options. They never select women for certain positions. And so, I decided to change the game and I became a management consultant.

Now I am feeling less and less the weight of these prejudices, but it scares me the number of I still see around me, still too many unresolved issues are scaring about men and women roles.

My daily struggle was and still is aimed to safeguard a heuristic principle: "If I know how to do a thing, (whatever it may be), it means that I can do it and if one woman can do a thing, then all women can do it."

Women need to be warriors because someone invented the gender war. And this war is not only against women. It is a war against the human evolution.

UNIT 20

WOMEN WARRIORS IN SOCIAL ENTERPRISE

BECOME MORE CREATIVE AND CREATE A SOCIAL ENTERPRISE

These are businesses driven by social or environmental purpose. They take on a kind of business structure that helps to show to the outside world they operate with a social purpose. They deliver goods or services that have a social purpose and any profits made. Yes, you can make a profit; you can reinvest this back into the business to drive forward its social purpose.

Examples – THE BIG ISSUE and Divine Chocolate; Eden Project; Jamie Oliver's Restaurant 15; Women Like Us, etc. There are considerable Fair Trading Companies that are SE.

They are not driven by the board of directors or trustees to draw down funds for personal use from the profit. You aim to maximise profit for the SE to grow! Profits can be made from the business via supplying the community with goods or services or other businesses.

Examples – Health and social care; renewable energy; recycling; retail; employment to sport; housing to education, etc. It is about putting something back into the community that drives a Social Enterprise (SE).

I have had a SE and drove forward WORKBIZ CLUB to encourage local people to join groups, to support local jobs for local people and to give them a platform and the tools to do this (www.ccoworkcic.com). You can have a social objective within your business. This normally is the impetus to drive the business forward to make a profit to be reinvested back into this model to create sustainability and bring about a positive change.

HISTORY OF SOCIAL ENTERPRISE

Since the 1840s, a cooperative worker's organisation was set up to provide food at affordable prices, because factory conditions and their workers were being exploited. Then in the 1900s cooperatives, SE and voluntary organisations started to take off.

GROWTH

Since November 2009, it has been found through a survey that an SE, as compared with an SME, is twice more likely to succeed and turnover is considerably better than for SMEs.

WOMEN-FRIENDLY

SE challenges the "glass ceiling," and 26 percent are women-led. More than 1.3 million people consider themselves to be SE and they attract 35 percent of all new SMEs, who are true entrepreneurs, as opposed to in the UK 2015 where only one in five are women-led in general.

REASONS TO HAVE A SOCIAL ENTERPRISE

Over 60 percent of a survey in 2007 found that local people would rather that SE provided the support of services to their community than public or private sector companies. Thirty percent of people would rather work for an SE than in any other industries.

You can be successful. From running a bike shop to having an IT consultancy to helping people with disabilities, the choice is yours!

You need to make a profit to compete in the available market. This enables you to become independent and not rely on public funds/grants. It also propels you to provide solutions to what is needed within your community.

CIC – COMMUNITY INTEREST COMPANY

I found by far the easiest way forward in 2010 was to create the above—hence, wwwccoworkcic.com. It is a legal structure created specifically for SE and is now recognised by banks. Indeed, RBS/NATWEST takes the lead on this and is presently asking for submissions for grants from £3k to £10k. It is regulated, so the organisation cannot deviate from its social mission or objective and its assets are protected. You can use most your profits for the objective of a social enterprise and in that way, protect your business.

SOCIAL ENTERPRISE MARK

From February 2010, this was created and you can aspire to achieve this mark through your local Social Enterprise Network or Coalition. Visit your local Social Enterprise Coalition website for support and guidance at www.socialenterprise.org.uk.

THE MOTHERSHIPGROUP – LIVERPOOL

In March 2015 at the Growth Conference in Liverpool, I heard a lady speak called Lorna Davidson and she gave me some of her valuable time over a coffee. I was inspired by her workshop and wanted to know more. From sitting down with Lorna, I could see that she was genuine and comfortable in financing, she managed small micro businesses and helped them to develop and grow.

Established by CEO Lorna Davidson, the business has five other directors who are all successful entrepreneurs. They all share a passion for creating innovative, customer-centric propositions rooted in the values of delivering mutual benefit and doing the right thing for their teams, customers and suppliers.

I had the pleasure in the summer of 2015 of having a coffee with Lorna and was so at ease in her presence and felt a real calm. Lorna has inspired people to live their dreams, as well as living her own. I felt so confident in Lorna's company that I have invited Lorna to work in partnership with us for 2016.

In just eighteen months, The Mothership Group has launched four new business propositions, a marketing agency and a charity and directly employs fifteen people in Liverpool.

The Mothership Group's unique location within Liverpool's Baltic Creative provides a vibrant entrepreneurial community, giving employees the opportunity to collaborate, share ideas and challenge established thinking.

The directors are committed to providing employees with opportunities to learn, grow and develop by taking on new areas, expanding the boundaries of their roles. All employees work across the various businesses that form the group, giving them a wide breadth of knowledge and expertise.

UNIT 21

GREAT BRITAIN – WOMEN WARRIORS THROUGHOUT THE CENTURIES

When I first came up with this title, I was immediately taken back to Boudicca.

BOUDICCA FACTS

Known for: British Celtic warrior queen who led a revolt against Roman occupation

Dates: 61 CE

CHANGING FORTUNES

Boudicca's army had counted on seizing Roman food stores when the tribes abandoned their own fields to wage rebellion, but Suetonius had strategically seen to the burning of the Roman stores. Famine thus struck the victorious army, weakening them.

Boudicca fought one more battle, though its precise location is not known. Boudicca's army attacked uphill and, exhausted and hungry, it was easy for the Romans to rout them. Roman troops of 1,200 defeated Boudicca's army of 100,000, killing 80,000 to their own loss of 400.

I would dispute here that a woman who was so brave and who had been through torture, war and seeing her daughters raped would take her own life rather than face the same people that she had faced many times previously. Also, I see this as a coward's way out and Boudicca was not a coward. So I will dispel this as nonsense and believe that she died in battle a hero, or lived to a happy old age.

QUEEN ELIZABETH I

Elizabeth I, the last Tudor monarch, was born in Greenwich on 7 September 1533, the daughter of Henry VIII and his second wife, Anne Boleyn.

Elizabeth succeeded to the throne on her half-sister's death in November 1558. She was very well educated (fluent in six languages) and had inherited intelligence, determination and shrewdness from both parents.

MY PERSONAL VIEW OF QUEEN ELIZABETH I

I can vividly remember studying her in my last year in primary school in Capel, Kent and I was asked to make a doll to resemble her. I cheated and had my Grandmother Isabella put the outfit together. I used to look at her in the history books and even went to visit Hampton Court, as I became so intrigued by her and the Tudor Dynasty. To me, she was very pale, with red hair and little, tight features and she always looked so unloved and unhappy. She also looked very cross all the time. This queen is probably remembered for giving up a personal life for the good of her country—very admirable and what a sacrifice for a woman at the time. There have been many women who have made this sacrifice to be at the top of the career ladder, or even for the success of their business and I know personally how that feels. I would like to let you know that I made Elizabeth I a beautiful canary yellow silk outfit or my grandmother did, as she needed cheering up and it then brought her to life more for me and I was as a child able to look at more as she then seemed more glamorous.

I chose not to marry my childhood sweetheart, though he was and still is a great person and has made a most amazing dad, as I wanted a career—to travel and experience life and that I did. So was that selfish of me, as Queen Elizabeth I was given this label? Though in your career you keep putting it off and putting it off and then hey bingo your biological clock has stopped ticking and there are no more eggs.

Today is Mother's Day and I had a workout. I swam and looked around me in the swimming pool at all these little children splashing around and their parents floating with delight and pride. I was jealous but knew it was my choice, so I only had myself to blame. Then a friend's husband came rushing in with his little girl, Izzy, who I had two nights earlier been dancing with in her grandmothers' lounge. The roles have changed, as there seemed to be more fathers taking their children swimming than women, or had the men allowed their partners a lie in for Mother's Day?

WOMEN WARRIORS IN THE MIDDLE AGES – HISTORY AS PROOF

When doing some research for this book and relating to its title, I made a little history walking through of proof that women were warriors—and from all accounts were so good at it, it begs to ask why, then, when we think of great leaders we think of men? It is because men have written most of the history books and were probably our history teachers. My first recall of any role model was my Grandfather Bert, who I was told had been a pilot in the Second World War, but he was not. I feel that this was made up not because he was a coward and did not go to war, but was needed at home tending to the land – though he did when he retired took up flying and indeed got his Pilots' license. Though my father, Jonny Gould had been in the British Army as it was National Service in those days and he did win some medals for bravery and he always spoke about his great adventures fighting the MAW MAW in Africa and I was convinced that was what I was going to do. I quickly went off that idea when we were on route to Australia and visited South Africa and witnessed at first hand 'APARTHEID' and it felt so wrong and we were as a family all uncomfortable with that including my father. My brother then was coached by my Mother to have a career in the Navy – she used to take him down to Portsmouth every weekend – he even had a Teddy bear as a baby that had a sailor suit on. Then when my mother realised that she needed to make his dream come true of being in the Navy or was it hers – my brother went away to board at the Navy College in North Wales, which is not there anymore. Unfortunately, when my Brother met his wife who is today home on leave in Blackpool he did not continue with this career though he always informs me that he greatly regrets that.

FEMALE WARRIORS IN THE MIDDLE AGES

Female warriors, duellists and military commanders of the Middle Ages (5th – 14th century)

Piracy between the 5th and 9th centuries was predominately a male activity, but there is a minority of historical female pirates, especially during the Norman or Viking period.

5th century CE – Princess Sela was the sister of Koller, King of Norway. She was a skilled warrior and pirate. She fought against King Horwendil and was later killed by him c. 420 CE.

529 CE – Princess Halima was the daughter of King al-Harit and princess of the Ghassan kingdom. In an act of revenge, she led a battle against the Lakhmids, who had sacrificed her brother to their goddess.

530 CE – Tomyris was the leader of an Iranian nomadic tribe called the Massagetae; her exploits were recorded by historians like Herodotus and thus passed into legend. Her stories, however, have been recorded both in history books and in paintings. The Persian Emperor of the time, Cyrus (the Great) attempted, unsuccessfully, to subjugate the Massagetae. He decided to entrap the Massagetae by leaving a camp full of wine; the Massagetae, now drunk, allowed the Persians to attack with little resistance and were captured. One of the captured was Tomyris's son; when he realised his mistake, he committed suicide. Tomyris was so furious at this deception she demanded a fight on equal grounds with Cyrus. Her wish was granted and she led a successful army that slaughtered the Persians, with Tomyris chopping off the head of Cyrus, which she apparently then kept and used as a wine glass.

535 – 552 CE – In the Gothic war Procopius writes of an English princess, referred to as "the Island Girl." She is said to have led an invasion of part of Jutland, where she captured the young King, Radigis, who had jilted her after their betrothal.

590 CE – The Christian Synod of Druim Cett ordered that British women should no longer go into battle alongside their men. This ban probably had little effect and traditions such as sword dancing, which was taught by women, remained.

1149 CE – The Order of the Hatchet, also called the 'Orden de la Hacha' in Catalonia, was a military order of knighthood for women, founded in 1149 by Raymond Berger, count of Barcelona. The honour given to the women was for the defence of the town of Tortosa against a Moor attack. The "Dames" received many privileges with the honour; these included exemptions from all taxes and they took preference over the men at public assemblies.

c. 1157 – 1247 CE – Tomoe Gozen was a rare Japanese samurai warrior, known for her bravery and strength. She fought alongside men in the Genpei War of 1180 – 1185.

c.1160-1213 CE – Tamar, Queen Regnant of Georgia, though she was a woman, is always mentioned in Georgian history as King Tamar. Tamar was the first woman to rule Georgia in her own right. Under her rule, Georgia achieved military superiority in the Middle East. A brilliant military tactician with a loyal army behind her, she led the men into battle and endured the hardships of an ordinary soldier. She could neutralise repeated invasions on her own nation, whilst conquering parts of Turkey, Persia, Russia and Armenia.

The 13th century sees trial by combat/judicial duels between men and women becoming more commonplace, particularly in Germany and Switzerland. It was used in Germanic Law to settle accusations, often with the absence of confession or witnesses and was often used in rape cases. For the duels to be judged as fair, the man was placed into a pit up to his naval, whilst the women freely moved around it. Weapons of choice included singlesticks, leather belts and fist-sized rocks that were wrapped in cloth. There were rules for the duellists: If either of the participants' hands or weapons touched the ground, they were considered the loser and paid the penalty. For women, it was the loss of the right hand and for men, it was beheading. There were many different types of trial by combat/judicial duels and they remained in use throughout the Middles Ages, slowly disappearing in the 16th century.

1236 – 1272 CE – Eleanor of Provence was Queen Consort of England and the wife of Henry III of England. Eleanor was completely devoted to Henry and when Simon de Montfort tried to rebel against him, Eleanor raised troops in France for Henry's cause. But Eleanor was not particularly liked in England, mostly because of her bringing so many of her relatives, known as "Savoyards," to England and then putting them into influential government positions. She was especially hated by Londoners; this hatred was returned. When her barge was sailing down the Thames, it was attacked by the citizens of London. In retaliation, Eleanor demanded from the city all back payments on a monetary tribute (queen gold). Eleanor received one tenth of all fines collected. She went even further in her revenge campaign by levying other fines on citizens on the thinnest of pretexts. This fuelled further anger against her and the citizens then pelted her with stones, mud and vegetables, forcing her to take refuge at the Bishop of London's home. When Henry died, she remained in England as Dowager Queen and eventually retired to a convent.

And we could not leave this history lesson without mentioning ***JOAN OF ARC***

Not just a legendary female warrior but also a Roman Catholic saint, **Joan** was but a girl when visions of the Archangel Michael drove her to approach the military of France's King Charles VII and offer to assist in his efforts to expel the occupying English in the later days of the Hundred Years' War. Though initially mocked by these men and soldiers, Joan was taken seriously once her influence ended the Siege of Orleans in nine days.

By age seventeen, she played a key role in commanding France's army and her forte in the military seemed to be strategy rather than slaying. The French owed much to Joan and yet it was the Burgundians, Frenchmen loyal to England, that led to her demise. She was captured in 1430 and, despite several escape attempts and rescue efforts, Joan was put on trial by the English for heresy and cross-dressing. Her visions were now derided and her armour called an atrocity. She was convicted, sentenced to death and burned alive at the stake.

Even after her death, her strategies are said to have influenced the French battle model. More than twenty-five years later, the Catholic Church revisited Joan's trial for heresy, overturning the charges against her in a case of too little, too late. It would be more than 460 years before Pope Benedict XV declared Joan a saint.

Can I ask the question: If the Catholic Church had not been ruled and were not still ruled by men, then would Joan have had the charges against her dropped sooner?

UNIT 22

WOMEN WARRIORS TAKE ON THE WORLD ECONOMY

THE ECONOMIC EMPOWERMENT of women and the rise of the entrepreneurial economy are two defining trends of our time.

In this report, the Centre for Entrepreneurs has partnered with Barclays to unravel how gender influences entrepreneurship, with a focus on the perspective and experience of women entrepreneurs. This provides us with a better understanding of what women face in their first year of business, beyond the start-up phase and considering the future.

This report is compelling because the findings shatter the stereotypes that many of us hold about the entrepreneurs who are growing businesses and powering the UK economy: The women in this research show stronger entrepreneurial ambitions than their male counterparts.

But there is more to do.

Whilst there has been significant growth in the number of women rising to C-suite executive levels and companies have adopted policies to boost the number of women on professional boards, we need to address the barriers to entrepreneurship for women. Currently, women are underrepresented in business creation, not just in the UK, but globally.

We need more women entrepreneurs because their role in fostering prosperity is clear. They are not only achieving higher profits and taking home a higher income than their male counterparts, but they also demonstrate a commitment to growing a profitable business and providing stability for their employees.

Our hope is that this in-depth look at women in business will provide policymakers, investors, the media and entrepreneurs themselves—as well as those considering such a move—with the evidence to look beyond the stereotypes regarding what makes a successful entrepreneur.

FOREWORD SIAN HANSEN EXECUTIVE DIRECTOR OF THE LEGATUM INSTITUTE NON-EXECUTIVE DIRECTOR OF THE CENTRE FOR ENTREPRENEURS

Entrepreneurship brings huge value to the UK economy, driving growth, jobs and innovation and helping to foster the kind of export mentality the UK needs to succeed on a world trade stage.

The number of new businesses in the UK in the last six months of 2014 increased by 3.7%. and is expected to rise; therefore, it is vital the emerging entrepreneurial economy is supported. Banks play an important role; with the specialist support, we can help business owners to bring their ambitions to life.

As a bank and indeed for society in general, it is important to understand what motivates businessmen and women, what challenges they face and what lessons we can learn from their approach to business that can be shared more widely for future growth.

The latest studies show women are still underrepresented in business, leading only 19 percent of the UK's small and medium enterprises. Barclays is actively engaging with businesswomen and committed to providing the support they require to achieve their ambitions. This report examines how positive commercial and societal impact can be created by better understanding the needs of businesswomen and supporting the growth and expansion of their business. The results provide a real insight into their motivations, the drivers for success and how their approach and incentive to achieving it differs from men.

Identifying the different behaviours of female and male business owners is imperative and enables the industry to create an optimum environment to support this valuable economy, which in turn will boost economic growth.

"At Barclays, we are passionate about helping businesses to grow, from start-up to multinational. It is always a personally rewarding experience meeting clients and working with them to deliver solutions that will help achieve their business ambitions."

FOREWORD FROM BARCLAYS JOHN WINTER CHIEF EXECUTIVE OFFICER CORPORATE BANKING

Barclays Entrepreneurship Index March 2015

Headline Findings

Though it is often assumed that women want to run "lifestyle" businesses, both men and women showed a strong appetite for growing the businesses they own or manage.

- Ninety percent of men and 92 percent of women who are executives stated that they are very or extremely interested in growing their business in the next three years.

- Among entrepreneurs, 82 percent of men and 83 percent of women report being very to extremely interested in growing their business in the same time frame.
- Perhaps because they are more concerned about sustainable growth, women are more aware of potential barriers to growing their businesses and mitigating risks compared to their male counterparts.
- Although men and women cited the same top barriers to growth, women cite twice as many barriers.
- Women are underrepresented in entrepreneurship globally. Yet women showed greater entrepreneurial ambitions than their male counterparts in this sample of professionals.
- Less than 18 percent of male entrepreneurs say they are very or extremely interested in starting another business in the next three years, compared to more than 47 percent of female entrepreneurs.
- Sixty-nine percent of female C-suite executives are very or extremely interested in starting a business in the next three years, compared to 29 percent of their male counterparts.
- Moreover, women and men equally rate their business skills, but women are more likely to see the need to acquire more knowledge or skills and the reach of their networks as barriers to growth.
- Twenty percent of women report their knowledge of markets as insufficient compared to 9 percent of men.
- Seventeen percent of women report that their technical knowledge was lacking, compared to 5 percent of men.
- Twenty-seven percent of women saw the strength and reach

of their networks as an obstacle, compared to 9 percent of men.

We polled and interviewed just over 500 C-suite executives and entrepreneurs from UK businesses reporting an annual turnover more than £2 million, spanning a variety of sectors and industries. Women explained that they are as growth-oriented as their male counterparts, but characterised the execution of growing their business in a different way. They strive for steady, profitable growth trajectories, often preferring to reinvest business profits over equity investment to scale sustainably and tend to think of male entrepreneurs as more concerned with fast growth and a quick exit.

THE STATE OF PLAY

The number of active companies in the UK increased by 3.7 percent in the second half of 2014 to form almost 3.1 million companies, the second highest rise in the past three years. The UK's start-up activity remains very strong, with total early-stage entrepreneurial activity (TEA) in the UK rising to 8.6 percent of the working-age population (18 to 64 years), up from 7.3 percent in 2013.

Record numbers of women are now in the British workforce, following an increase of nearly 800,000 over the last four years. More women than ever before are on the boards of the UK's largest companies, with the FTSE 100 on track to hit a quarter female representation this year.

Looking at the profiles of the businesses we surveyed, we found the women to be younger and running newer businesses. Female entrepreneurs were eighteen years younger than the median male entrepreneur in our sample and the businesses led by women are seven years newer than the median of the male-led businesses. But there is still a long way to go. According to the most recent OECD data, there is a gender gap of almost 50 percent in entrepreneurship in the UK. Among those either in the process of starting a business or running a new business, the rate for women was at 7.5 percent in 2014, lagging the rate for men, which was 13.5 percent.

Women-led small and medium-sized enterprises already add £70 billion to the UK economy. As they scale up, it is imperative that we recognise women who are entrepreneurial role models to help fill the remaining gaps.

Two macro trends are in play: a rise in the number of people entering entrepreneurship and women continuing to increase their economic clout.

BOTH MEN AND WOMEN SHOW A STRONG APPETITE FOR GROWTH

We asked this group about their ambitions to grow their own business (or the businesses they lead) and found both men and women show a strong appetite for business growth, with no significant gender differences. Ninety percent of men and 92 percent of women who are executives say they are very or extremely interested in growing their business in the next three years. Among entrepreneurs, 82 percent of men and 83 percent of women report being very to extremely interested in growing their business.

During our research, we found that there is a perception that women run "lifestyle" or "kitchen-table" businesses, but aren't serious about growth. Though such entrepreneurial activity is undoubtedly rising in popularity and is to be encouraged, our data shatters the assumption that women-led companies aren't interested in scaling up.

WOMEN SHOW A GREATER RANGE OF GROWTH AMBITIONS

The research explored the areas of how entrepreneurs and executives are interested in growing their business. Among entrepreneurs, women show a greater range of growth ambitions, including both domestic and international growth and through the entry of new products and price points.

SHATTERING STEREOTYPES

To understand the attitudes and aspirations of those poised to be founders of successful businesses, or already leading a growing enterprise, we have focused our research on a highly successful group of C-suite executives and entrepreneurs. They are those who have made it beyond the start-up phase of the business lifecycle and are running an established firm. This allows us to understand their journey, from the challenges in their first year of business, to beyond their first million and looking to the future.

In what ways are you interested in growing your business/ company in the next 3 years?

Both the entrepreneurs and executives were asked about their entrepreneurial ambitions. We found that less than 18 percent of male entrepreneurs say they are very or extremely interested in starting another business in the next three years, compared to more than 47 percent of female entrepreneurs.

This greater appetite for entrepreneurship flies in the face of stereotypes. It can be interpreted as either a greater desire among these highly accomplished women to start a business, or it could be evidence of an ambition gap where men are more likely to have leapt into entrepreneurship and women are held back by barriers. In fact, although men and women cite the same top barriers to growth, women report a higher number of barriers. These will be discussed in more detail later in this report.

FEMALE ENTREPRENEURS EARN MORE THAN MEN

When looking at the median wage of all workers in the UK, women still make 19.7 percent less than men. Yet there are signs that entrepreneurship is bucking this trend. Previous research supports the existence of a reverse pay gap among entrepreneurs, where women are out-earning their male counterparts. It found that female entrepreneurs earn 17 percent more than their male counterparts. By contrast, among executives, women were making 21 percent less than men.

In our sample, we replicate this finding. The median income showed women entrepreneurs take home twice that of men. We report these findings with caution, as they conflict with most research on gender pay gaps. However, this does appear to be clear evidence that entrepreneurship provides women with an opportunity to break through the perhaps ingrained barriers in other sectors.

Overall, we found that both men and women in this group are ambitious about growing their businesses soon. Both are interested in starting another business or making the entrepreneurial leap from the corporate world. However, women show higher rates of interest in starting a business (or another business), especially among C-suite executives. But this report isn't just about ambitions. In the next sections, we will examine some of the factors that enable entrepreneurs and executives to grow their business and better understand how gender issues can help or impede them.

DELUSIONS OF GENDER

A study from Harvard, the University of Pennsylvania and MIT looked at the role of gender in entrepreneurial pitches. They played hundreds of identical pitch presentations to groups of investors but changed whether they had a male or female narrator. When investors were asked to pick which ones they thought would be successful, male narrated presentations were 40 percent more likely to be picked to receive funding than those narrated by women. In a follow-up experiment, evaluators particularly favoured pitches from "attractive" men, whereas attractive women were perceived worse than both "unattractive" men and women.

People expect entrepreneurs to have certain qualities and behaviour's, such as risk-taking and an ability to innovate. But these same characteristics may be valued differently when displayed in men versus women. Take two examples.

RISKY OR RECKLESS

Women are proud of their approach to risk. Today, women are seen to be more risk-averse than men and there is evidence to support this perception. Economic experiments estimate women are 20 percent more risk-averse than men. Risk-taking and over-confidence are the two most persistent gender differences across numerous studies. However, there is a danger in making assumptions across the board. Female financial professionals, e.g. fund managers, have an appetite for risk more like that of men. Similarly, the women in our survey of executives and entrepreneurs rate themselves slightly higher than men on statements like "I am a financial risk-taker" and "People I work with would say I am fearless in the face of failure."

In the 18th and 19th centuries, wealthy aristocratic women were often investors, speculators and gamblers. These were risky activities and risk-taking was associated with women and femininity. Risk was described as "a woman's lack of self-control" and their propensity to act on "irrational whims." As financial dealings became formalised through the 19th and 20th centuries with protocols and regulations, the stereotypes around gender and risk shifted and men have predominantly filled these roles.

92% of women report that they are good at both identifying and mitigating risks, compared to 88% of men. 80% of women say they see opportunities where others might see risk, with 67% of men reporting the same. 87% of the women in this group see themselves as financial risk takers, compared to 73% of men. 91% of women and 86% of men report that others would describe them as fearless in the face of failure.

When talking about taking risks, the women we interviewed were proud of their ability to take calculated risks, but they also tended to judge risk differently than men. They are more sensitive to risk and cite it as a barrier to growing their businesses. Twenty-four percent of women said it was a bad time to take on risk due to personal finances, with only 6 percent of men reporting the same. Eighteen percent of women will report that a risk is unlikely to pay, compared to 6 percent of men.

What are the obstacles you see in growing your business? (Approaches to risk)

Male 6%

Male 6%

Male 8%

Bad time due to poor finances

Risk is unlikely to pay

Don't see a promising opportunity

Female 24%

Female 18%

Female 13%

However, men and women in this sample seem to calibrate success differently. Just as men were less likely to worry about risks in the environment, when asked to rate the success of their business over the past three years, male entrepreneurs were highly skewed towards "prospering" while female entrepreneurs showed a roughly normal distribution, with a slight skew towards "struggling." This difference is particularly striking because the women-owned businesses in our sample were not struggling more than businesses run by men. On the contrary, the women-owned businesses happened to have higher profit before tax.

It's important to ask why this might be. Arguing that women are less confident and that men are over-confident is simplistic. The women in this sample did not lack confidence. In fact, they showed a high level of confidence, one even going as far as to refer to herself as a "genius."

Investors should be alert as to how over-confidence and conversely a lack of the same can skew business owners' perceptions of the health of their businesses. They must calibrate success potential with objective measures, rather than rely on perceptions.

As mentioned previously, the women interviewed said they take a different approach to risk and growth than how they think of male entrepreneurs. They explained that they are as growth-oriented as their male counterparts, but characterised the execution of growing their business in a different way. One woman in our research said:

Often, the women said they take a calculated approach to risk, consider multiple factors for growth and aim for controlled growth. They perceive their growth trajectories to be steady and tend to think of male entrepreneurs as more concerned with fast growth and a quick sell. The exit stage didn't seem to be on their radar.

Words like "aggressive" and "gung-ho" were used alongside assumptions that male entrepreneurs could act recklessly.

So, what's normal? How should entrepreneurs judge business health or approach risk? It is problematic that we calibrate confidence and risk-taking using a masculine norm. Speaking at the First Women Summit, a panellist argued that women entrepreneurs "don't over-promise and then under-deliver." If this is true, it was apparent from the women we spoke to that they did not want to be judged on gender expectations, but business success. This requires the public, policymakers, investors, the media and entrepreneurs themselves to fight any remaining biases about both men and women pursuing entrepreneurship.

There is a need to recognise that entrepreneurs are not a homogeneous group and there are different but still successful, models of growth. Women are quite willing to take risks, but they are also more sensitive to risk and this vigilance can be an asset.

Additionally, they talk about planning, managing and controlling growth: When describing their growth ambitions, women used different words to describe their business goals versus how they perceived men's business goals. They used familial words and nature imagery and talked about the freedom provided by entrepreneurship to talk about themselves. According to __, "there's a lot of talk about high growth and, generally, that puts women off because it's a bit blokey, it's a bit .com-y and I think women are more concerned about sustainable growth."

These are some examples of the women's use of imagery:

"Would I make a decision that risks the entire company? No, that would be a bad risk."

"I have to think about his [co-owner's] livelihood… I could get out now if I was by myself."

"Growing is the most important thing, but profitable growth."

"It's got to be managed growth, profitable growth that's achieved in a way that doesn't knock people off their perches."

"[My business] is like a child growing up… It was about turning the baby into a teenager."

"… grows organically"

"It's happened naturally. It's a product that arrived quietly."

"It's not money that matters, it's freedom."

The women interviewed said they consider a wide range of factors when it comes to growing their business. Many focus strongly on corporate responsibility and their contribution to society and their local area. Very few are willing to risk staff for the sake of growth. They explained:

Women see themselves as growing their businesses but in a different way. Women see more barriers. In addition to unconscious bias, women may experience additional barriers when starting and growing a business. There is a need for nuance and to understand that women have strong growth and entrepreneurial ambitions while recognising they see and experience barriers to growth.

31% TEAM CAPABILITIES

27% High level of competition

23% ALREADY DEALING with rapid growth

22% Difficulty accessing capital

What are the obstacles you see in growing your business?

Although men and women cited the same top barriers to growth, women cited more obstacles. On average, male entrepreneurs cited 2.7 barriers, whereas women cited 4.6.

WOMEN WANT TO BUILD THEIR KNOWLEDGE AND THEIR NETWORKS

Both executives and entrepreneurs were asked about barriers to growth relating to their soft skills, technical skills and areas of expertise. Though women rated their business skills as highly as men, they were more likely to see insufficient knowledge as a barrier to growth. For instance, 20 percent of women report their knowledge of markets as insufficient, compared to 9 percent of men. Seventeen percent of women report that their technical knowledge was lacking, compared to 5 percent of men. Across almost every type of skill or knowledge area, women saw up-skilling themselves to furthering their business.

Women are interested in building their competencies in

several areas. Interviews revealed that women want a solution-oriented education. Later we will discuss the types of education and support that are in high demand from women. Networks can be an enormous source of knowledge, or at least a means to contact the right hire to fill a competency gap. When asked about their network, 27 percent of women saw the strength and reach of their networks as an obstacle, compared to 9 percent of men.

Though there has been an explosion in women's networks, which has been a great asset for women, this might not be a sufficient. Interviews revealed that women found great difficulty finding women's events in which they could network with industry leaders. In our sample of successful women, only 33 percent of their key mentors and influencers were other women. This figure was only 3 percent among the men. Given this, high-level entrepreneur networks must include experienced, influential men and women if women are to advance. Increasing the visibility of successful women at entrepreneurship events could have a great impact on perceptions around gender and entrepreneurship. For instance, it's important for both men and women to see high-achieving women on public panel debates.

Therefore, those who provide this kind of support should see events geared specifically toward women as an important first step, but focus efforts on achieving a 50:50 gender balance in the wider entrepreneurial networking community.

What are the barriers you see in growing your business? (knowledge and networks)

Male 9%

Male 5%

Male 9%

Knowledge of new markets

Technical knowledge

Strength of network

Female 20%

Female 17%

Female 27%

Fig 12.0

BEYOND BUSINESS, THERE ARE LIFESTYLE FACTORS IN PLAY

As you would expect, women are more likely to cite childcare as a barrier to growth, though this is not as high as you might expect—only 17 percent. Women are also more likely to support their spouse's business endeavours, both in terms of time and financial commitments and are three times more likely to cite this as an obstacle when they are starting up their own businesses (5 percent of men vs. 24 percent of women).

In 2016 in the UK 4/5 new start ups were women led businesses and in Spring 2017 I have been invited to sit on the Board and support a new Women led Angel Academy started by 2 Australian female Entrepreneurs with an office in London and in 2017 Manchester to only seed fund female led businesses so there is change out there to support women and I have been steering this vehicle for years it seems.

SUPPORT FOR ENTREPRENEURS

To help make their ambitions a reality and overcome barriers to growth, we asked executives and entrepreneurs about their interest in various types of educational and networking events and services. Most emphasised that support must be personalised. Relevance is also key for entrepreneurs—they want to meet people from similar sectors or business sizes who are facing similar problems. There is a big difference between females in micro businesses and those running enterprises like those in our research. In fact, they can be sceptical (and even hostile) to being grouped with women if this includes smaller businesses they share little in common with.

Our survey found that both men and women are interested in networking events, industry-specific roundtable discussions, members-only business networks and educational seminars. Interestingly, men showed a preference for a board of advisors and consultants for advice, whereas women showed a preference for coaches and mentors for education. There is a slight and subtle difference here that should be kept in mind by service and support providers.

Again, supporters should understand that in the scale-up phase, women focus on long-term sustainability of the business, not simply rapid growth to position themselves for exit. Education and networking support are as important as access to funding. They should also ensure networking and roundtables have appeal by making them relevant to sector and business size and being solution-oriented. Because some entrepreneurs prefer "consultation" and some prefer "education," those who provide event and support services for entrepreneurs should think about the language used so they are not exclusionary.

Furthermore, support should recognise the need to encourage women specifically, but without singling them out as women. The overwhelming majority of the women interviewed felt that acknowledging their gender diminished their accomplishments, i.e. suggested that they were successful for a woman. Similarly, they felt special services for women implied that they might need help because of their femaleness. This is a delicate balance. One entrepreneur explained:

"It's always nice to meet other female entrepreneurs, but should a financial package be tailored to just one sex? No, I don't think it should."

Additionally, this audience can be sceptical (and even hostile) to being grouped with women if this includes a smaller business that they share little in common with. For instance:

"I don't really think about the fact that I'm a female. I know I've won a couple of awards for females in business, but I've decided not to enter any more competitions that are just female. I really think I should be compared to everybody and I don't see why I shouldn't be."

A CALL TO ACTION

Policymakers, investors and funders, the media, entrepreneurs themselves—as well as those considering entrepreneurship—should:

- Assume women have strong growth ambitions while recognising that they see and experience more barriers to growth.
- Adjust for biased perceptions about the ambitions and competence of women.
- Be alert to how over-confidence and lack of same can skew business owners' perceptions of the health of their businesses. They must calibrate success potential with objective measures rather than rely on perceptions.

- Understand women are quite willing to take risks, but they are also more sensitive to risk and this vigilance can be an asset.
- Recognise that entrepreneurs are not a homogeneous group and that there are different but still successful, models of growth.

ENTREPRENEUR SUPPORT AND SERVICE PROVIDERS SHOULD:

- Understand that in the scale-up phase, women focus on long-term sustainability of the business, not simply rapid growth to position themselves for exit. Education and networking support is as important as access to funding.
- Ensure events and seminars have appeal by making them relevant to sector and business size and making them solution-oriented.
- Be mindful of the language and style adopted, so as not to be exclusionary, because some entrepreneurs prefer "consultation" and some prefer "education."
- See events geared specifically toward women as an important first step, but focus efforts on achieving a 50:50 gender balance in the wider entrepreneurial networking community.

The women we researched stressed that it was essential to treat them based on business achievements rather than on gender expectations. When considering support for entrepreneurs to start and grow a business, we ask all stakeholders to generate activity around entrepreneurship that is gender intelligent. We make the following recommendations:

And finally, there is a reason to celebrate. Women-led small and medium-sized enterprises already add £70 billion to the UK economy.

As they scale up, it is imperative that we recognise and support women who are entrepreneurial role models to help fill the remaining gaps in entrepreneurship.

UNIT 23

WOMEN WARRIORS IN DISGUISE

I WAS READING THE BOOK, *IN SEARCH OF THE WOMAN WARRIOR*, by Richard J Lane/Jay Wurts, while on a chill out break with my BBGF Sheila. It explores the Amazons and the modern Amazons, Molly Frith, as an example under UK King Charles reign, she was a 'landlocked privateer' and though she dressed as a man and had the courage of a man, I do not feel that imitating men are necessary to be a successful entrepreneur. The book goes on to discuss 'RADIGUNDS', one being Edith, who went on to running her own business for grant proposals for mental health, etc. Edith searched for role models and found this in Eleanor Roosevelt. What I observed is that with power comes conflict and then you don't become that 'HAPPY ENTREPRENEUR' or have that mindset. So, I would not want any greater power than to inspire and motivate other entrepreneurs to become successful, but not at a price.

An example of a Woman Warrior who has overcome so much is ALISON ABRUNEIRAS, a survivor of cancer. Read more . . .

Thousands of Brits have turned to eBay to save or make a few pounds, but not many can say that it has helped them in making a fortune.

Alison Abruneiras runs a successful business grossing more than £1 million a year after becoming addicted to the auction website. Incredibly, the forty-six-year-old mum left school with no qualifications or business experience.

Alison was making just £70 a week as a nail technician when breast cancer forced her to stop working altogether. But, after logging on to eBay in her bedroom at home as a fun 'hobby' to take her mind off the treatment, she's become a hugely successful entrepreneur.

In six years, her cosmetic retail business, the Nail and Beauty Emporium, has grown to become a big hit on eBay. It now trades worldwide and Alison has had to expand into a warehouse and take on four staff, including her twenty-two-year-old daughter, Coralia, who is set to take over the business.

Alison, from Lincoln, said, "Looking back, it's incredible to think that this all started with my computer in my bedroom. It has been hard work, but I'd like to show other people that it can be done. If I can do it, anyone can. Anyone can earn money. You don't have to have an education; I don't have a GCSE to my name."

Alison has had an interest in business since childhood. At eleven years, old, she was given a little market stall by her shopkeeper dad to sell washing-up liquid and other small items. But she never pursued her talent. At the age of twenty–one, she moved to Lanzarote, Spain. After falling in love with her now husband, Amador, who is forty-seven and working as a holiday rep and nail technician. The couple had their children: Coralia; Amador, twenty-one; and Luis, fifteen, before moving back to the UK in 2005, where Alison continued work as a nail technician.

At the age of thirty-eight, she was forced to give it up after being diagnosed with breast cancer. For the next two years, she underwent agonising treatment, including a lumpectomy and mastectomy. Her ovaries and lymph nodes were removed before she began a course of chemotherapy. "It was a huge shock to me," Alison said. "When you're diagnosed with something like that, it knocks you off your feet. I lost a lot of my confidence and became incredibly depressed."

With spare time on her hands, Alison turned her attention to eBay. She explained, "I didn't want my whole world and life to be about cancer and chemo and that's how I discovered eBay. I wanted a hobby. I needed something to take me away from that hell, something to focus on. At the time, eBay was my focus and it was exciting. "I started by buying a foot spa from an end-of-line shop and seeing if I could sell it for a profit. I bought it for £10 and within a week, I'd sold it for £30. I would be checking the internet every half an hour. Making that sale gave me that buzz and made me feel good. I didn't think about whether I was going to die or whether the treatment was going to work." "Everything was a real whirlwind, but building my business gave me a way of fighting cancer. Then, when I'd finished the treatment, I was left with an empty void and I was wondering what I was going to do next. That's when my business really took off; I put everything into it after that."

Boosted by her newfound sales talent, Alison used her expertise as a nail technician to expand into other cosmetic products. "I bought £3,000 worth of products from a wholesaler and stored them in my bedroom, which had become my office. Within two weeks, I'd nearly sold all of that, too. "From there it became an addiction. I'd be on the computer first thing in the morning and up until midnight." The business proved a real lifeline when Amador lost his job as a restaurant manager in 2010. Alison said, "My hobby suddenly became the only income and I knew we were going to have to make it a success to survive. Amador started working with me and we worked together for two years. He put some really good things in place and we made it work."

Three years ago, Alison went from sole trader to a limited company and today her business continues to boom, expanding to the websites Amazon and Play. But, despite all her success, she remains incredibly grounded and lives a modest lifestyle. At her three-bedroom rented home, you won't find designer clothes and flashy cars. In fact, the only luxuries Alison enjoys are family holidays to Florida and Egypt and a brand-new camper van. She's also treated Coralia to a brand new Mini as a reward for working so hard. She said, "My daughter has taken a leaf out of my book. Like me, she didn't do very well at school and left with no qualifications. But she's proving a real whizz when it comes to business. Everything she knows is self-taught. She's amazing on social media and all the suppliers love her." Alison has now set her sights on the hospitality industry and has opened a Spanish Tapas restaurant, called Ole Ole, next door to the family home. Under the management of Amador, it has also become a huge success in just five months, already rated fifth best of 335 restaurants in Lincoln on TripAdvisor. Alison concluded, "We have worked like crazy and life has completely changed but it's changed for the better.

I can relate to this as Alison overcame adversity and turned a negative into a positive. What started out as a hobby has turned into a million-pound business. Not only that, she is self-taught. She never gave up and always believed in herself, though not educated, nor did she attend any business school or read books on the subject. What I love about Alison is that she then went on to support her husband, who himself was made redundant and faced the uncertainty of a future and now they own a Spanish Tapas restaurant that is rated fifth best of 335 restaurants on TripAdvisor in Lincoln.

I was not so long ago faced with another failing business, poor health and having to have time out of my business to try and turn it around to support my mother who had breast cancer. Then to top it all, my husband was made redundant after a serious accident at work and we had to move home to support my mother and downsize our home. It took eighteen months to support my husband in finding a new career starting out as a kitchen porter with a famous restaurant chain and now he is on their Head Chef Academy and I no doubt will be supporting him to start his own Italian restaurant. I never gave up believing in myself and others never stopped believing in me. So, thank you to my husband, friends and colleagues who supported me through this challenging time.

UNIT 24

WOMEN WARRIORS WHO DISRUPT

EMMELINE PANKHURST WAS A LEADING BRITISH WOMEN'S RIGHTS ACTIVIST, WHO LED THE MOVEMENT TO WIN THE RIGHT FOR WOMEN TO VOTE.

Emmeline Goulden was born on 14 July 1858 in Manchester into a family with a tradition of radical politics. In 1879, she married Richard Pankhurst, a lawyer and supporter of the women's suffrage movement. He was the author of the Married Women's Property Acts of 1870 and 1882, which allowed women to keep earnings or property acquired before and after marriage. His death in 1898 was a great shock to Emmeline.

In 1889, Emmeline founded the Women's Franchise League, which fought to allow married women to vote in local elections. In October 1903, she helped found the more militant Women's Social and Political Union (WSPU)—an organisation that gained much notoriety for its activities and whose members were the first to be christened "suffragettes." Emmeline's daughters, Christabel and Sylvia, were both active in the cause. British politicians, press and public were astonished by the demonstrations, window smashing, arson and hunger strikes of the suffragettes. In 1913, WSPU member Emily Davison was killed when she threw herself under the king's horse at the Derby as a protest at the government's continued failure to grant women the right to vote.

Like many suffragettes, Emmeline was arrested on numerous occasions over the next few years and went on a hunger strike herself, resulting in violent force-feeding. In 1913, in response to the wave of hunger strikes, the government passed what became known as the "Cat and Mouse" Act. Hunger-striking prisoners were released until they grew strong again and then re-arrested.

This period of militancy was ended abruptly on the outbreak of war in 1914 when Emmeline turned her energies to supporting the war effort. In 1918, the Representation of the People Act gave voting rights to women over thirty. Emmeline died on 14 June 1928, shortly after women were granted equal voting rights with men (at age twenty-one).

I must ask the question here if the war had not broken out and needed women to fill the gap in jobs that were normally taken by men, from warehouse to factory work and so on, would the vote for women have been delayed until the next war of 1939?

UNIT 25

ETHNIC WOMEN WARRIORS

MADAM WALKER

"I am a woman who came from the cotton fields of the South. From there I was promoted to the washtub. From there I was promoted to the cook kitchen. And from there I promoted myself into the business of manufacturing hair goods and preparations... I have built my own factory on my own ground."

Madam Walker, National Negro Business League Convention, July 1912

Madam C.J. Walker was born Sarah Breedlove in 1867, the first child in her family born into freedom after the signing of the Emancipation Proclamation. Her parents and five older siblings were slaves on a plantation in Louisiana. By the time of her death in 1919, Madam Walker was the wealthiest black woman in America and the first self-made female American millionaire.

Sarah's parents died when she was only seven years old and she moved in with her sister and brother-in-law and soon began working to help support their family. She married when she was fourteen to escape her brother-in-law's abuse. Her husband died when Sarah was twenty, leaving her to raise their two-year-old daughter, A'Lelia, by herself. Sarah began experiencing hair loss at a young age. Hair loss was a very common problem at the time: People found it difficult to bathe and wash their hair as often as we do today because most lacked access to things like indoor plumbing, central heating and electricity. Sarah began experimenting with different products and home remedies, eventually creating her own shampoos and hair treatments. She named her company after her husband at the time, Charles Joseph Walker and began selling products such as "Madam Walker's Wonderful Hair Grower" and "Madam Walker's Vegetable Shampoo." Designed specifically for black women, her hair products were completely unique at the time. She began selling her products door-to-door and teaching the women she met all about hair and scalp treatments.

Her business was so successful that she was soon selling her products across the United States. Sarah's daughter, A'Lelia, ran a mail-order business from Denver while Madam Walker travelled the states, finally settling in Indianapolis, where she opened her own factory. After establishing her headquarters there, she expanded her company internationally to Jamaica, Cuba, Costa Rica, Panama and Haiti. Her company employed thousands of people, including many African-American women and was the largest African-American owned business in the nation.

Not only was Madam Walker able to create an incredibly successful business against all odds, she also used her wealth to oppose racism and support institutions to assist African-Americans. She said that she wanted to be a millionaire not for herself, but for the good she could do with it

This woman truly inspires me, as I am so in awe of women who rose against all the odds against her as a woman, who was also black, from a poor background, abused and uneducated. Walker travelled all over the USA to set up her business because she believed it was a solution to her own personal issue with losing her hair. Walker used her money to support education with you black men, women and children.

This is one of my favourite Women Warriors. Do you know someone who needs to be recognised? Send me a line and photograph at karen@gateway2enterprise.co.uk.

UNIT 26

SHAPING A WOMAN WARRIOR

THIS SECTION IN MY BOOK was sparked by a comment my mother made to me on Mothering Sunday 2015: "As a child, you made adults nervous, as you came out with statements that most children would not dare to say!" My mother told me that I could walk and talk by the time I was six months old and was very independent and was in the nursery by the time I was eighteen months—though maybe this was because my little sister came along. The nursery was at the bottom of our garden and instead of walking around using the footpath, I found out that the quickest route was to climb over the garden fence. Once in 2012 at an interview in Liverpool for a CEO role, I was told by a board mainly made up of male members that I made them nervous because I worked out of the box, I replied, "No—I move the box to get the job done!" And this was evident when I went to nursery.

At nursery, I noted that little girls were left to play with dolls. I did not play with dolls and I love being outdoors, so I found that the most interesting activity for me in the summer months was the sandpit and building objects. I was not fazed by noting that this sand pit was taken up with little boys—indeed, I jumped straight in, grabbed their toys and began building my empire.

When I was at primary school, which was a local village school that was in South England in the commuter belt of Kent in Hilden borough. Even though my father was a local sportsman and gifted horse rider, I was still treated as a second-class citizen. One of these reasons is that I was not a little cute girl who liked playing in the Wendy House, making tea and playing mummy; I used to escape the classroom and wonder around the Rec, exploring nature, which was a lot more interesting. Another reason was that the school was very focused on a "class divide": 50 percent of the children came from the Cold Harbour Lane area, with their enormous homes and gardens and some from the new wave of wealth that commuted to London on the new Goff Cooper Estate. Though we owned our own home, it was on a Council estate and my Father's family lived in a Council House, which they went on to own and my Grandmother had been in service as the Cook for local gentry and my Grandfather, a Groom in Service again with local Gentry. So, though my father was a brilliant rider and had served in the British Army in Africa and was honoured with medals and had his own building company, his twin Danny had resided down the road had had a brush with the law and they had six children and lived in a part of the village as being certainly very working class.

It was no noted that I was bright; indeed, when I was only five and we were asked to write up what we did at the weekend, my stories were so vivid I was called a "liar" by the teacher and my mother was summoned to the school. Yes, I always had a vivid imagination, but my weekends were never dull with parents like mine. After school on a Friday night, I would, on my own, at the age of five, take the bus from Hilden borough to Tonbridge with my weekend bag packed. I would then sometimes be met by my aunt and wait to take another bus to my grandmother on my mother's side, some 5 miles away. It was here at weekends I could be free and enjoy the activities that I enjoyed. I was encouraged to read and write by my grandfather Bert, who was self-taught and who went on to write poetry. I was left to roam the countryside on my own or with the local boys—not girls, as little girls played with dolls and I did not. So, I played war games to win with the local little boys.

At this primary school, we had a headmaster there who I knew to keep away from, as my grandmother on my father's side had advised me that this man had a habit of putting his hand in little girls' knickers. She was very outspoken and how did she know this? Well, her daughter went there. I noticed that in gymnastics he always insisted on helping us little girls over the hobby horse and I observed that his hand always managed to be around the knickers area. So, I decided to avoid this activity, though I was dying to jump over that horse and do one of my Arab Springs that I had been practising in my back garden. I would refuse and stand there in defiance. He summoned me to his office for a punishment. Once in his office, I told him why I had refused! I can't remember his face, as he was a tall, withered man with a pitched face and these round specs—he had a mean face. He went as red as a hot poker and puffed up his face and his shoulders and I thought he was going to slap me there and then. But no—I escaped and had no more trouble with him, so then I could show off my talents on the hobby horse. He also did not question when sometimes on a Friday afternoon in the summer my father would leave work early and just waltz into the roasting classroom and tell the teacher that I was leaving, as we were off to the seaside. What a relief.

Then my mother announced that we were emigrating to Australia for a better life. At the time I hated her for this and the one person I missed was my Grandmother Isabella. But boy, Australia gave to me what I needed—the freedom, adventure, sports, creativity in the classroom and so much more. What an experience, but sadly my mother, from the day we landed, decided it was not for her, as she could not adapt to their culture. But for me and my father, it was ideal. At my primary school at Cog gee Beach, I was put on a pedestal as in the classroom; I always sat in the top four places in the classroom, because of my weekly test results and my sports achievements, I secured my place to being the Captain of the Netball team, the Rounder's team, the Swimming team and the Athletics team, Australia was paradise for me to learn and train. Then in the afternoon what more could a curious, naughty child want more than to explore the beach, go swimming and surfing and enjoy the great outdoors and come in late.

Upon returning to the UK, we lived with my mother's parents, which was ideal for me. I was enrolled in a local, small-minded village primary school, Capel; the school was run by a husband and wife team who owned this amazing large house, their son Richard was in my class. Because of my Aussie accent, I was ridiculed, picked on and called some very nasty names, which did hurt then. So my grandmother thought that if I had some elocution lessons, this would help. Unfortunately, the lessons did not help; I thought I could use my strengths to play against them. In the classroom, the opposite of what the school thought, I was not behind in any subject and indeed sat on the top table with the Headmaster's son Richard. On this table, there were four of us preparing for the 11 plus and grammar school. Of course,

Richard went, as well as his friend, whose parents were wealthy friends of the headmaster and then another girl, whose family was also wealthy. They all went to grammar schools; I was passed up, but that never stopped me. I also realised that my sports ability would beat the bullies, so I threw myself into all activities that I excelled at. I remember that I so much wanted to be in the Choir, but they told me NO, that I could not sing, but that did not stop me attending, I used to sit there and listen and wait my turn and they, of course, used to rub it in, they never did let me join. But I never gave up and just by sitting there this used to put the off, as I never went away.

Happy Days of my sister and myself I was 16 dreaming of becoming an Actress in 1976 in our garden.

I had to get this in my book, as I dreamt about this last night. Why? Because my husband had been demoted at work after having two weeks off with chicken pox as a chef at a very famous restaurant chain. I told him on his first day back to go in there and show him what a great chef he is and never give up. He went in and was put on the pasta section; from his signature dishes that day, the restaurant had many compliments. This was brought to the attention of the manager and finally, my husband spoke up, as I am always encouraging him to speak up for himself. Modesty is great, but don't stand there and be a wallflower. The manager then informed him that maybe they had not been fair in their decision and would discuss this with the GM. My husband finally endorsed the fact that his culinary skills brought them compliments and that when he had been off, they received complaints. He came home and walked in the door ten feet tall and he then believed in himself again. Therefore, you must never give anyone the power to take away from you what you are good at—and we all have many things that we are BRILLANT at!

UNIT 27

WOMEN WARRIORS IN MUSIC

I CANNOT LIVE WITHOUT music and it has given me so much pleasure in life. From an early age, I was introduced to the jazz greats, from Ella Fitzgerald to Billy Holiday to Nino Simone to Sarah Vaughan, by my father's mother, Mrs Gould. I never knew her first name, as that is what we had to call her. She was quite a striking woman—very tall, so not a natural beauty, but she always knew what she wanted. I used to go with Mrs Gould to buy records in Woolworths with her and then we would put them on once back at her home, with all the kids, animals and neighbours that popped in. Mrs Gould would encourage me to dance to the music and it gave her real pleasure to see me dancing around the living room while she was having her hair done, with a sherry in one hand, dictating her orders of the day to my Grandfather Ted.

I particularly related to these Women Warriors of music, as I felt their pain in their journey. It gave me comfort as I matured that other women suffered in silence and were in pain; I was not alone and I could drive this pain into a positive force.

ELLA FITZGERALD

Ella Fitzgerald, known as the "First Lady of Song" and "Lady

Ella," was an American jazz and song vocalist who interpreted much of the Great American Songbook. I always found that Ella turned her pain in hope and happiness when she sang.

Following a troubled childhood, Ella Fitzgerald turned to singing and debuted at the Apollo Theatre in 1934. Discovered in an amateur contest, she went on to become the top female jazz singer for decades. In 1958, Fitzgerald made history as the first African-American woman to win a Grammy Award. Due in no small part to her vocal quality, with lucid intonation and a broad range, the singer would go on to win thirteen Grammys in total and sell more than 40 million albums. Her multi-volume *Songbooks* on Verve Records are among America's recording treasures. Fitzgerald died in California in 1996.

EARLY YEARS

Born on April 25, 1917, in Newport News, Virginia, singer Ella Fitzgerald was the product of a common-law marriage between William Fitzgerald and Temperance "Tempie" Williams Fitzgerald. Ella experienced a troubled childhood that began with her parents separating shortly after her birth.

With her mother, Fitzgerald moved to Yonkers, New York. They lived there with her mother's boyfriend, Joseph De Silva. The family grew in 1923 with the arrival of Fitzgerald's half-sister Frances. Struggling financially, the young Fitzgerald helped her family out by working as a messenger, "running numbers," and acting as a lookout for a brothel. Her first career aspiration was to become a dancer.

After her mother's death in 1932, Fitzgerald ended up moving in with an aunt. She started skipping school. Fitzgerald was then sent to a special reform school but didn't stay there long. By 1934, Ella was trying to make it on her own and living on the streets. Still harbouring dreams of becoming an entertainer, she entered an amateur contest at Harlem's Apollo Theatre. She sang the Hoagy Carmichael tune "Judy" as well as "The Object of My Affection," wowing the audience. Fitzgerald went on to win the contest's $25 first place prize.

BILLIE HOLIDAY

Billie was probably one of my favourites, to this day, of the great jazz singers. I related to her songs and the humour and honesty and I liked to sing along with her, as I too have had issues with bad relationships with men and demons with drink and drugs in the past. Billy always opened her heart to her audience and sang about her recent pain in the song "The Man I Love." Being so brutally honest with her audience about being beaten by her lover, I feel, made Billie take about domestic abuse.

Early Life

Jazz vocalist Billie Holiday was born Eleanora Fagan April 7, 1915, in Philadelphia, Pennsylvania. Considered one of the best jazz vocalists of all time, Holiday had a thriving career as a jazz singer for many years before she lost her battle with substance abuse. Her autobiography was made into the 1972 film *Lady Sings the Blues*. In 2000, Billie Holiday was inducted into the Rock and Roll Hall of Fame.

Holiday spent much of her childhood in Baltimore, Maryland. Her mother, Sadie, was only a teenager when she had her. Her father is widely believed to be Clarence Holiday, who eventually became a successful jazz musician, playing with the likes of Fletcher Henderson. Unfortunately for Billie, he was only an infrequent visitor in her life growing up. Sadie married Philip Gough in 1920 and for a few years, Billie had a somewhat stable home life. But that marriage ended a few years later, leaving Billie and Sadie to struggle along on their own again. Sometimes Billie was left in the care of other people.

Holiday started skipping school and she and her mother went to court over Holiday's truancy. She was then sent to the House of Good Shepherd, a facility for troubled African American girls, in January 1925. Only nine years old at the time, Holiday was one of the youngest girls there. She was returned to her mother's care in August of that year. According to Donald Clarke's biography, *Billie Holiday: Wishing on the Moon*, she returned there in 1926 after she had been sexually assaulted.

In her difficult early life, Holiday found solace in music, singing along to the records of Bessie Smith and Louis Armstrong. She followed her mother, who had moved to New York City in the late 1920s and worked in a house of prostitution in Harlem for a time. Around 1930, Holiday began singing in local clubs and renamed herself "Billie" after the film star Billie Dove.

NINA SIMONE

I came across Nina Simone later in my teens during a time at school when I had a history teacher who was trying to convert me to communism; I joined the Anti-Nazi League and went on protests and demonstrations in London. Nina was the Lady of Jazz who did just that, who took on the issue of racism. Though Billie also did this in one of her songs about the lynching of black men in the South of USA, it was Nina who took on this mantle and even sang at Martin Luther King Jr.'s funeral. It was now in my early teens that I listened to many black artists from a wide range of music, from Jazz, Blues and Soul to Motown, R&B and Reggae. I would dance across the UK in dance competitions and still do to this day, as I always wanted to be a professional dancer but was stopped by my height. Still, it does not stop me at every opportunity, as I love dancing the night away with friends.

Nina was one of the most extraordinary artists of the twentieth century, an icon of American music. She was the consummate musical storyteller, a *griot* as she would come to be known, who used her remarkable talent to create a legacy of liberation, empowerment, passion and love through a magnificent body of works. She earned the moniker "High Priestess of Soul," for she could weave a spell so seductive and hypnotic that the listener lost track of time and space as they became absorbed in the moment. She was who the world would come to know as Nina Simone.

When Nina Simone died on April 21, 2003, she left a timeless treasure trove of musical magic spanning over four decades.

Clearly, Nina Simone was not an artist who could be easily classified.

Nina was deeply affected by these two events. In 1962, she had befriended noted playwright Lorraine Hansberry and spoke often with her about the Civil Rights Movement. While she was moved by her conversations with Hansberry, it took the killing of Medgar Evers and the four girls in Birmingham to act as catalysts for a transformation of Nina's career.

There were many sides to Nina Simone.

These feisty Women Warriors of jazz pioneered the way for women of today in music, from Taylor Swift to Beyoncé and they took on board domestic violence, racism, equal rights and more. They identified with the pain of some women and reached out to them in music and were not ashamed to wear their heart on their sleeves, as I do. Their music does not make me sad or depressed but gives me comfort that we are here for the common cause of supporting other women, whether in business or the community, as family or friends.

UNIT 28

UNDISCOVERED WOMEN WARRIORS

First Women, The Collection, is about women's achievements and one woman's exploration through the camera lens that endeavours to answer the question: How will women be remembered over the past 100 years? What have they achieved in the fields of Sport, Science, Politics, the Arts and Education? And who were these remarkable "first" women, what did they look like?

Lt. Becky Frater RN: The first woman to pilot a Black Cat helicopter.

Sarah Outen: The first woman to row solo across the Indian Ocean.

Charlotte Budd: The first woman to ride in the Grand National (1977).

Abbey Burton: The first woman to set a British record title of 100 percent perfect score in Olympic Trap Clay Shooting.

WOMEN IN POLITICS

Baroness Scotland: The first woman to be attorney general.

WOMEN IN MUSIC

Clio Gould: The first woman to lead the Royal Philharmonic Orchestra.

WOMEN IN POLITICS

Baroness Helene Hayman: The first woman to be Lord Speaker.

UNIT 29

THE "NEW" WOMEN WARRIOR

TAYLOR SWIFT

A TALENTED SINGER/SONGWRITER and a real feminist heroine, Taylor was voted in the Top Ten Most Powerful Women in 2015. She took on Apple over their refusal to pay royalties to musicians. It is the time for change and this young woman is a strong role model in charge of her own destiny—that is what makes her a Woman Warrior.

Taylor Alison Swift (born December 13, 1989) is an American singer/songwriter and actress. Raised in Wyomissing, Pennsylvania, she moved to Nashville, Tennessee at the age of fourteen to pursue a career in country music. She signed with the independent label Big Machine Records and became the youngest songwriter ever hired by the Sony/ATV Music publishing house. The release of Swift's self in 2006 established her as a country music star. Her third single, "Our Song," made her the youngest person to single-handedly write and perform a number-one song on the Hot Country Songs chart. She received an Artist nomination at the 2008 Grammy Awards. In 2015, Taylor Swift has become the youngest woman ever to be included on Forbes most powerful women list, making it to number 65.

Swift's second album, *Fearless*, was released in 2008. Buoyed by the pop crossover success of the singles "Love Story" and "You Belong with Me," *Fearless* became the best-selling album of 2009 in the United States. The album won four Grammy Awards, making Swift the youngest ever Album of the Year winner. Swift's third and fourth albums, 2010's *Speak Now* and 2012's *Red*, both sold more than one million copies within the first week of their U.S release. *Speak Now's* "Mean" won two Grammy Awards, while *Red's* singles "We Are Never Ever Getting Back Together" and "I Knew You Were Trouble" were worldwide hits. Swift's fifth album, the pop-focused *1989*, was released in 2014. It sold more copies in its opening week than any album in the previous twelve years and made Swift the first and only act to have three albums sell more than one million copies in the opening release week. The singles "Shake It Off," "Blank Space," and "Bad Blood" have all reached number one on the *Billboard* Hot 100.

Swift is known for narrative songs about her personal experiences. As a songwriter, she has been honoured by the Nashville Songwriters Association and the Songwriters Hall of Fame. Swift's other achievements include seven Grammy Awards, twenty-two Billboard Music Awards, eleven Country Music Association Awards, eight Academy of Country Music Awards and one Brit Award. She is one of the best-selling artists of all time, having sold more than 40 million albums—including 27.1 million in the U.S.—and 100 million single downloads. Swift has also had supporting roles in feature films, including *Valentine's Day* (2010) and *The Giver* (2014).

I think she is the modern "Woman Warrior" because, as a young lady in the music industry with tremendous pressure on her to conform, she took on Apple in June 2015 and won!

As giant missteps go, Apple's stumble was at least quick and somewhat gracefully caught. Today, the world's second-largest technology company announced that it had experienced a sudden change of heart about its controversial plan not to pay royalties to record companies during the three-month trial period of its new paid-for streaming service. That this news came not via an official statement, but a Twitter message to Taylor Swift only added to the startling nature of what we were witnessing: the humbling of a major corporation by a 25-year-old woman. Less than 24 hours earlier, Swift had made her feelings about the payment policy clear via an open letter on her Tumblr. Explaining why she had refused to allow the company to stream her latest album, *1989*, she wrote:

I find it shocking, disappointing and completely unlike this historically progressive and generous company. Three months is a long time to go unpaid and it's unfair to ask anyone to work for nothing. We don't ask you for free iPhones. Please don't ask us to provide you with our music for no compensation.

The hours rolled, the outrage grew and then the company responded: "We hear you @taylorswift and indie artists," they tweeted. "Love, Apple."

Swift, far from being a David to Apple's Goliath, is a phenomenal force in today's music industry. This week's triumph over Apple has revealed Swift to wield a clout that many other major artists and labels do not. She was, after all, not a lone voice in the music industry. The British independent label Beggars Group—home to Adele and FKA Twigs—had also set out its concerns: "We struggle to see," it wrote in a statement, "why rights owners and artists should bear this aspect of Apple's customer acquisition costs." It's worth mentioning that Elvis Costello referred to Swift's Apple letter as "a note from our future president."

Swift is a very particular figure in the world of entertainment. She notches up remarkable sales—in terms of her album sales, her live performances and her merchandise—but she is set apart from her peers by an almost old-fashioned sense of poise. This is not some Disney-whittled starlet with an inevitable drink and drugs meltdown looming on the horizon, her songs a wearisome routine of latex and thrusting. Rather she is canny, strikingly demure, in control of her own career and, it should be noted, author of her own songs.

That public persona has been well honed. Her early reputation was perhaps a little wet—she was a girl with a guitar, known for penning winsome songs about failed romantic relationships. When Kanye West stormed the stage at the 2009 VMAs to protest her triumph over Beyoncé in the best female video category, the world leapt chivalrously to the defence of this crestfallen young woman in the glittery dress.

But since then, Swift has been gathering strength. She has acquired a carefully curated entourage of female celebrities, many of whom were unveiled in the video for her recent single "Bad Blood" as a sort of superhero force: from Lena Dunham to Ellie Goulding, from Jessica Alba to Cindy Crawford and Cara Delevingne.

Her songwriting has evolved, too, revealing a sense of humour and self-awareness. Her recent single "Blank Space" poked fun at her reputation as a serial dater. "Got a long list of ex-lovers," she sang. "They'll tell you I'm insane / Because you know I love the players / and you love the game." The accompanying video, meanwhile, parodied her princess image with a run of ball gowns, mansions and ponies.

Pop is a fickle business; its star's wax and wane. Yet Apple's climb-down this week suggests a faith in Swift's longevity as an artist. It's also illustrative of a shift in the entertainment industry. Recent years have seen a rise in strong female performers such as Swift, who baulk at the notion of conforming or compromising and who have had no qualms about questioning accepted notions of female beauty, behaviour and sexuality. Or even, when the need arises, calling out multinational technology corporations.

New Women Warriors of 2016/2017 who dare to speak up – true story Karen Richards Mentee – Transgender

I first met Karen when she bravely pitched to me when I was Director of the Rock Star Program NW for Start-Ups UK 2016 where I personally mentored and supported over 2000 start-ups.

February 2012 was the most traumatic period of my life; I have just walked out of the relationship which I have been in for over six years into unknown territory.

Armed with only a bag of clothes and an elderly dog for company I was moving into a semi-derelict house with no job and my mind set on a pathway that could easily destroy my career.

Simple fact I was 46, with a long-established work record in the construction industry, a person of high workplace value and in high demand.

The truth was I wasn't happy and I was living a lie about who I was. I had always been a woman, only in male packaging. It was time to be true to me.

My ex had scorned me "if you do this you will only be able to get a job stacking shelves at the local supermarket or selling your body (as if anyone would pay for it) at the back of Manchester Piccadilly train station".

I had felt like I was in the wrong body since I was about six, but in those days, it was shunned upon being gay, if I'd have come out as a transgender person, I may well have been killed.

It is estimated that gender variance affects as many as 1% of the UK population, however, there are only about 8000 of us that have fully transitioned. Most become social outcasts and I knew this more than anyone. I did what most do, overcompensate by throwing myself into the most masculine things, building, rugby, motorbikes and the pub, this also left me unable to form real relationships and certainly not ever express myself for years I described myself as a cross between an alcoholic and a workaholic, only facing my demons when I was in my early thirties.

I eventually moved from my native Yorkshire to Manchester in 2002, where I was determined to find myself, I joined a social group for trans people such as myself.

Things didn't go to plan as they seldom do, I met my ex on a dating site in 2006, we got engaged, moved in together and had at least the first two years of happiness. She always knew about my condition but didn't know how deep it ran. I didn't either.

For many years, I had been my own boss and at my ex's request I took a project manager job with a nationwide Shopfitting company, I hated it and although it was well paid on paper the company was struggling due to the 2008 credit crunch and the recession.

I left in 2009 and went freelance as a project/health and safety manager. I muddled through for a few years and while I had my freedom, my ex still wanted me to be a slave to the wage.

Now here I was 46 and at what I thought was the lowest point of nowhere. I had to be me, it was all or nothing.

I started job hunting and quickly found I was being offered interviews but these were quite quickly withdrawn when employers, discovered my gender status and the implications it may have on their company. In fact, I was treated as a joke. After several months, I decided to retrain in the construction health and safety sector which was something I had dabbled in before, this would not only elevate my Profile but would give me the opportunity to run my own consultancy, which was the best option as it looked like no one would give me employment. Convincing the jobcentre to assist me was the beginning, firstly they needed to realise I was not a normal case, which is difficult in a welfare system that thrives on turning people into drones for big corporations. Fortunately, they listened.

I got my NEBOSH qualifications later that year and applied to do a PTTLS course to support this which would also allow me to facilitate training. All this in the first year and in this time while still out of work I filled my time with making my home more habitable.

Unfortunately, the next stage of my plan fell to pieces as the job centre was forced to transfer me to a job facilitating company which had no experience in start-up business.

During this time, I was contacted by a friend from my past life who was recruiting a construction contracts manager and while this was tempting we both decided that due to my circumstances it would be better if I came on board as an external safety consultant. I still didn't have the funding to start the business and although this contract was out there, I couldn't start.

Months followed of futile job searching, workshops and meetings with my facilitator and I was just banging my head against a wall, finally I put in a complaint and after a long conversation with the regional director of the facilitation company they decided to support me in exploring the avenues for funding, but their knowledge was quite limited.

During this time, I also found I had a lot of inner strength and the support of many the new friends I had by just being able to be myself, I took a voluntary position to become night event manager at Manchester pride, which led to benign asked to join the board of directors of the event company, a position I still hold.

The trick through all of this was to remain focused, busy and not allow myself to give in, I was already punching above my weight, but success builds on success and nothing was going to stop me.

Strangely I was referred to a company called franchising works in Manchester and although my business was not a franchise, the wonderful team knew where to signpost me this was the first time that I had heard of Rockstar youth and I was quite convinced that this old fossil would not make the criteria, but I was convinced otherwise.

This was a one-off chance to pitch and I had to have this right, fortunately, the offer of contracts was still open and there was a major high street brand associated with this.

So, after nine long months (my business pregnancy as I call it) I attended my first new business incubator in the centre of Manchester.

There were about 20 people pitching that day and welcoming and facilitating this was Karen Gould, who settled us down beforehand and made us understand the criteria required. I must admit I was quite nervous although I believed because of the background work I had done, I would be able to demonstrate that my customers were out there and the business only needed the finance. I have run companies before in the labour supply sector, with two failures and one successful one and up to that point I had never even considered the value of mentioning or as Karen described it the cherry on top.

Surprisingly my pitch went well and there many in the room with equally good ideas, but I did feel my presentation had an edge that I was dealing with robust High street brands and I was providing a niche service that was required by law and nobody seemed to like doing, this was assisted by the fact that I had already had my payment terms in place and agreed in principal.

I realised very quickly that my business plan had to be robust, solid and achievable.

To assist me as I am no accountant I engaged the help of a friend who used to manage the finances for Aberdeen council, this would be based on three years' targets had to be realistic.

My second session at Rockstar was all about the business plans, Karen had brought in two business financial consultants to mentor us and even my plan needed a few tweaks.

The big issue was now I felt not if I would be approved, but when, my contracts were due to go live in the first week in January and the clock was ticking.

To say I'm persistent is a slight understatement, it can be a downfall, but I had to be this way to get me to this far.

With my plan submitted, I was just waiting for approval, my planning was in full swing, the business was to be run from my home, a one-person operation for now and as I have always learned cash flow is the key.

The downfall of many companies in the construction sector is payment terms which are traditionally 90 days. I could not survive on these terms, so my services had to include something special, something the clients needed. Cash.

Most construction contracts include retention clauses which the client holds back around 15% of contract value, 10 % of this is released after the release of what are known as the O&M manuals and 5 % is held on latent defects which are usually released after 12 months.

This is usually the markup for the contractor for the whole project, so I worked out that if I could provide a service that also provided the essential manuals, it would be in their interest to give me better terms (10 working days).

My approval came through on the 3rd of December 2013, but this didn't mean the money was in the bank. My first project started at the beginning of January and I had to hit the ground running, unfortunately sometimes you must put the pressure on and with Karen's support this is exactly what happened, phone calls emails even social media played their part leading the funding coming through on Christmas Eve. Working over the holiday allowed me to be prepared. This was happening and this was going to work.

I engaged a website designer and began to look at company logos, I wanted everything to be clean crisp and professional and note and more I was realising that although the funding was helping, it was the mentoring that was the valuable tool. Being able to bounce ideas off someone with such vast business experience such as Karen, gave me the confidence and reassurance I needed.

The company Karerisk Ltd launched in the first week of January 2014, but unfortunately, my first contract was delayed by 3 weeks. During this time my accountant called me and asked if he and his partner could invest in the company, as he liked the idea and saw a future for the business, this also included his service to the business. I consulted Karen and we decided to do this as it would allow me to pay Rockstar off at a very early stage, not affect the business plan and build a credit rating for the business.

Rockstar was therefore paid off within 5 weeks, at a cost of about £20. I still had the mentoring and support from them but I was financially independent.

Customers just seemed to come from everywhere and within a few months I had completed five projects and built my client base to 2 main contractors and 7 subcontractors, money was coming in and I could take a wage for the first time in years. In the July of that year, I was also asked by a major high street brand if I would put a job description for an internal health and safety adviser for their construction department, this was a great honour and I was even more surprised when I was asked to apply myself. Yes, I was being headhunted. Again, I had to listen to my mentors as various things had to be considered such as my ongoing medical treatment, my life in Manchester and did I want to give up all I had worked for.

I decided not to apply for these reasons.

This was for the best as the legal requirements for the law changed in early 2015 and the role may have been redundant, this was also part of the advice I gave, - researched honest and to the point, leading to the client never went ahead with the role and continued with external consultation.

During this time, I was appointed as CDM co-ordinator to a project in the centre of Manchester for a large taxi firm, thought this I gained a connection with a Manchester based architect who despite a cold initial start our friendship and professional respect for each other grew, I know am the preferred H&S consultant to his practice.

2015 was the most challenging year so far, my Gender reassignment surgery was getting closer and I was under no illusion that this would not affect the business, potentially 3 months off work was not the prospect I was relishing, but it was something I had to do I couldn't be complete. Fortunately, I was informed in June of the impending operation and I had 3 months to prepare. I spent every spare moment ensuring everything was in place.

Firstly, I decided to form a supply alliance deal with one of my competitors, that they would cover my projects (site visits only) while I was in recovery, as I could be operational for most other tasks. This turned the competition into cooperation, which is still in existence and we do provide cover for each other during operations including sickness and holiday cover. This along with the surgery taking place in my traditionally quiet period meant that my clients although aware of what was happening would not notice any reduction in service.

On 19th of October 2015, I entered the operating theatre to finally ensure my body matched the person inside, four hours later against Dr's orders I was back at the helm.

The following months I struggled through by careful planning and a lot of help from friends and colleagues. I moved forwards and backwards in my health which suffered a setback on the Christmas Day. When I was admitted to the hospital unable to swallow food or liquid, this resulted in a four-day hospital stay, an endoscopy followed by a course of tablets to control a stomach disorder. By the first week of January 2016, I was nearly at the stage of calling it quits and that meant everything. This was the company and possibly my life.

I decided to take some time out in Spain to rest and recover and feeling a lot better I returned to the UK.

To my shock there was a letter from the hospital asking me to go see a specialist; I thought I'd been discharged, obviously not.

On attendance at Manchester Royal I saw Dr Wang, a very pleasant lady, who told me they had to do the tests again, this time looking for cancer. I was rocked to my very foundations, was all I'd been through, coming to nothing?

The next few weeks were even harder, lack of sleep, work kept coming and it looked like I was achieving the impossible.

Another endoscopy and the anxious wait finally came late April. All clear. I've never been so relieved.

My life was back on track, I never stopped working all through this and always delivered the plan now how to keep my work, home and other interests a lot more balanced, Karerisk continues to grow at 50% year on year and although I have a website, nearly all my work comes from word of mouth.

Risks and investment must be planned and calculated in any small business, however, with mentoring and advice from those who have been there, this is far more valuable.

Year three is going to be more interesting, more new clients and expansion are on the menu, again through planning and measured investment.

I was always taught that a man will do enough work so he doesn't get sacked, a woman must work twice as hard just to keep the job. I would say a transgender woman must work three times as hard, kick down doors and shake foundations. It's hard but it can be done.

I am one that does this.

I knew Karen was special from the first day she pitched to me. She was unfortunately in a very difficult group very male lead and some very stereotype characters and she handled herself with confidence and with respect. I so admire her how she has not only coped with starting/growing a business in a male-dominated industry but with her own personal demons. I wish her lots of happiness which she so deserves. It taught me to never judge and that deep down we are all the same trying to find ourselves within and our vocation in life. Reach out 'Women Warriors' and you will find a true 'Woman Warrior' like Karen in a much-unexpected corner of our community.

UNIT 30

CONCLUSION

I WAS HONOURED IN APRIL 2014 to be nominated and be in the finals of the www.business-rocks.com Innov8 Awards for Best Digital Creative Tech Start-Up and finals for Forward Ladies UK Best UK Start-Up 2015. You will be not surprised to know that I am the only female-led business in this category and the only woman over 25—nothing new there. We were also in the semi-finals of the Virgin Pitch to Rich 2015 and in the Diversity 2015 UK finals. I have also just been asked to be one of their speakers in October 2015 in Milan at a Women in Leadership Conference and have partnered as a speaker with a group of women who work in IT in the UK to support more women and encourage them to work in this field or start businesses in this field.

The UK is the best place in Europe and third best for female entrepreneurs to set up a business, according to research by the Global Entrepreneurship and Development Index GEDI. Yet only one in five is owned by a woman and women are a third less likely than men to set up a business, according to a report by the Department of Business BIZ UK. This premier league is led by the USA, followed by Australia—even Iceland is in the top seven.

Both Goldman Sachs and NatWest have a 10,000-women initiative to help women in developing countries set up their own businesses. There is a strong link between economic growth and women being financially independent. What is holding women back from becoming that Woman Warrior? A lack of confidence? Women all too often set up a business out a need to provide for their family and have flexible working conditions. And, once they take this big step, it is the isolation—the fear from within—that holds them back. If you have a support network of other Women Warriors, as I do, then you are in supportive hands.

The next step for me is to form my own investment syndicate for women for 2016. I am looking for investors to support this project; contact me with your ideas.

When you feel you are beaten and all your confidence is lost, this is what kept me sane in July 2015. I had attended a finance conference in Llandudno and had a little too much to drink on the evening, as I was under pressure to present to a potential investor from Singapore impressive stats of successful leads – deals brokered and Jon our CTO had phoned me the night before and shattered my hopes—even though I had worked my butt off the last three months, we had only done 32 deals. I could not believe it and even doubted his credibility—our system—and thought to myself, "After 150k of my investment, what next?" Then I had to meet my mother in another hotel for the weekend. I was feeling lost and was looking for someone to turn to for advice; though my mother is a great business woman, I would not ask her as she would want to tell me, "I told you so!" Then I felt insecure that she would be pleased that I had failed and boast about this to my sister and brother. So I kept it to myself. Though, it did not help that though I had been to the beautician that week as we were taking a coffee and the Waiter/owner who was rather young, but very dishy was trying to chat me up, which did anger her as she is used to having all the attention so she informed me that I had a long hair sticking out above my lip. Can you image the embarrassment, but I did not care at this point? Then we had the usual comments about my weight only 4 weeks to our holiday and you must pull out all the stops. Why not stop eating I thought. I was relieved that on the second day she decided that she did not want to stay on and return home as she was bored – it was raining – she did not want to go on the beach and there was no shopping and nothing to do. Relieved was I! Though she still texts me the following day to go shopping. You probably know the answer to that as I was feeling at an all-time low I choose to put myself through my paces at the gym, less pain. I don't do abuse and I had had enough. Also, that morning, my husband had made the comment, "Boy what did you eat in Wales – you look so bulky" Two things pulled me through this dark time.

The UK Women's Football Team the night before had beaten the Germans—even though we had lost the World Cup, we came out fighting with true British bulldog spirit. This gave me the strength to dig deep and find that resilience. Thanks, girls—I needed that as much as you did.

Then in the summer of 2015 another Woman Warrior of sport, Jessica Ennis-Hill, came back from motherhood and took on the world and won a gold medal.

British track and field star Jessica Ennis won a gold medal in the heptathlon at the 2012 Summer Olympics in London.

EARLY LIFE

British track and field star Jessica Ennis was born on January 28, 1986, in Sheffield, South Yorkshire. She was raised by father Vinnie Ennis, a Jamaican-born, self-employed painter and decorator and mother Alison Powell, a social worker.

Ennis developed an interest in track and field at a young age when her parents took her and her younger sister Carmel to a track event at Don Valley Stadium in Sheffield. She took to the sport immediately, drawing attention for her near-perfect hurdle technique at just ten years old. She soon met her future coach, Toni Minichiello and joined the Sheffield Athletic Club, winning the high jump competition at the National Schools Championships at the age of fourteen.

In addition to the hurdles, Ennis tried her hand at the heptathlon, a gruelling race combination of high jump, long jump, shot put, javelin, 100-metre hurdles and the 200-metre and 800-metre races. Throughout high school, she devoted much of her time to training and continued while studying psychology at the University of Sheffield, where she graduated in 2007.

FAMED HURDLER

Ennis first established herself as one of Britain's top young athletes in 2003, at the AAA U20 Championships, where she won both the indoor pentathlon and outdoor 100-meter hurdles. That same year, she began competing internationally, with the 2003 World Youth Championships in Canada, followed by the 2004 World Junior Championships in Italy and the 2005 European Athletics Junior Championships in Lithuania. In 2004, at age eighteen, Ennis won the 60-meter hurdles at the Northern Senior

Indoor Championships—her first senior tournament.

Over the next few years, Ennis continued to dominate track and field, eventually finishing fourth at the World Championships in Japan and second overall in the World Combined Events Challenge. In 2008, however, she faced major disappointment: A stress fracture in her right foot caused her to miss the 2008 Olympic Games in Beijing and sit out the rest of the 2008 season.

2012 OLYMPICS

Following a twelve-month break from competition, Ennis made a comeback in 2009, winning the world championships in the heptathlon and world indoor pentathlon title the following year. She shocked spectators when she won the 60-meter hurdles at a five-team international meeting in Glasgow, beating out indoor champion Lolo Jones. Under the guidance of her coaching staff, cleverly titled "Team Jennis," she continued her success in the following years, competing in her first Olympic Games in London in 2012.

At the 2012 Olympic Games, Ennis wowed audiences in the 100-metre hurdles (the first of her heptathlon events), setting a British record of 12.54 seconds. The time was the fastest any heptathlete had run the race since Jackie Joyner-Kersee's 12.69 seconds in the 1988 Olympic Games in Seoul. After a 1.86-meter high jump, a 14.28-meter shot put and a 200-meter personal best of 22.83 seconds, Ennis established a solid lead. Almost 36 hours after her first event, she finished the competition with the 800-meter. She secured the gold medal with a time of two minutes, 8.65 seconds and became the new Olympic heptathlon champion.

The other support I had that day was an article in the Sunday *Mail* about gratitude being the new humility, about how we forget to count our blessings; and so I did and then I had a great big smile on my face.

Next, I got back to the drawing board in my business and checked through all the statistics that my CTO had sent me and compared them with other stats, which confirmed that we had not done as well as I had hoped. But not all was lost as I called an urgent board team meeting. I will never give up on something I believe in and I believe in myself and won't allow others to take that away from me.

I wanted to leave you with the Forbes May 2015 Most Powerful Women in the World for you to digest. Send me your comments at karen@gateway2enterprise.co.uk.

UNIT 31

MOST POWERFUL WOMEN WARRIORS IN 2015

The world's most powerful woman, German Chancellor Angela Merkel, has a lot on her mind these days: Mediterranean migrants, Russian sanctions, home-grown spying scandals, Eurozone stability and the German wings crash, to name a few pressing issues. One thing she surely isn't thinking about, but we are, that come next year's U.S. elections, she could lose her title for the first time since 2010 to the one person with a credible and mathematical chance of "leading" the world.

Hillary Clinton has appeared on this *Forbes* ranking every year since it launched in 2004 as, in order, a senator, Secretary of State and influential personality. In 2015 Clinton is No. 2, just a breath and a ballot away from the Most Powerful Woman crown alas she was beaten in 2016 by new President Donald Trump, though he does have women in positions of influence supporting him.

This is *Forbes*' definitive annual audit of the foremost heads of state, iconic entrepreneurs and CEOs, as well as celebrity role models, billionaire activists and pioneer philanthropists, all ranked by money, media momentum, spheres of influence and impact (full methodology here).

This year's Top 10: Merkel and Clinton, followed by Melinda Gates, Janet Yellen, Mary Barra, Christine Lagarde, Dilma Rousseff, Sheryl Sandberg, Susan Wojcicki and Michelle Obama.

See Full Coverage of the World's 100 Most Powerful Women

The most powerful women in politics, philanthropy, business and tech are **Merkel, Gates, Barra and Sandberg**, respectively. Our top-ranking billionaire this year is **Oprah Winfrey** at No. 12, who has a personal net worth of $3 billion. **Ana**, the newly installed chair of Banco Santander, is the top woman in finance at No. 18. **Beyoncé Knowles** leads in the entertainment field at No. 21, while **Anna Wintour**, Conde Nast artistic director, reigns over the media sector at No. 28.

Read on for more highlights and click the slideshow to view the Top 25 Most Powerful Women:

2The concept of power can be nebulous—especially when it comes to gender. As of January 2015, ten women served as heads of state and fourteen as heads of government. Women currently hold twenty-three (4.6 percent) of CEO positions at S&P 500 companies. Of a total 1,826 global billionaires, 197 are women—11 percent of the total. Only 9 percent of executive officers in Silicon Valley are women.

That these wretched stats continue year after year is a serious and pressing issue. But there's hardly a void of powerful women—and the numbers are growing. If we enlarge our focus from only those who possess the greatest wealth or the heaviest corporate hammer to include the women whose influence the impact may be greater than the sum of their titles.

The headlines remind us whenever another woman gets the top job. Examples: GM's Mary Barra, Federal Reserve chair Janet Yellen, IMF head Christine Lagarde. But the fact that a great many of the women on this list are not the pointy head of the pyramid—such as Facebook's Sandberg and Nigerian Finance Minister Ngozi Okonjo-Iweala, or Gwynne Shotwell, COO of SpaceX and Apple's Angela Ahrendts—doesn't dim their enormous clout. They appear on this list because they illustrate a new math—it turns out you don't need to be No. 1 to be a Most Powerful.

The 2015 power women list features eight heads of state (plus one monarch) that run nations with a combined GDP of $9.1 trillion with over 600 million citizens, including the newly elected Polish Prime Minister Ewa Kopacz. The twenty-four corporate CEOs control nearly $1 trillion in annual revenues and eighteen of the women here founded their own companies or foundations, including our youngest self-made billionaire, Elizabeth Holmes, 31. Speaking of, this year's class has fifteen billionaires with the cumulative net worth of nearly $75 billion. The total social media footprint (Twitter, YouTube) of all 100 Power Women is nearly 475 million followers and fans.

Here is a quick peek at Power Women 2015: Business Club 2015 Newcomers: 19 is new to the list in 2015. Ana Patricia Botin, the new chair of Banco Santander, makes a strong showing at No. 18. Ana has now retired and I worked with her in Liverpool 2012 when Santander launched their Breakthrough Program in the UK. I took my Business Club to this Event to network and to meet such a great woman. Though I was not impressed with the way I was approached. Two of her male colleagues came over to me midway in conversation and insisted that Ana was ready for me now and to come now and I was then escorted over to her. We next met at the IFB2014 Business Festival in Liverpool where I had the Start-up Contract and they were one of the Sponsors and she wowed the audience again. In 2016 I have the contract for IFB2016 for gateway2finance and gateway2digtal for 29/30 June 2016 www.gateway2enterprise.co.uk join us.

Ana Patricia Botín-Sanz de Sautuola O'Shea, DBE is a Spanish banker. On 10 September 2014, she was appointed the executive chairman of Santander Group, the fourth generation of the Botín family to hold this.

Other names to know: Google CFO Ruth Porat, EU Foreign Policy Chief Federica Mogherini, power pop star Taylor Swift and top venture capitalist Jenny Lee of GGV Capital.

Hall of fame: Seven women who appeared on the inaugural list in 2004 are still here today: Melinda Gates, Christine Lagarde, Hillary Clinton and Indra Nooyi. Also, of course, Oprah, Queen Elizabeth II and Ho Ching.

She's No. 1: Chancellor Merkel has made the list ten times over the past twelve years—nine times as No. 1. She was first elected in 2005 and won a historic third term in 2013.

She's the first: Nearly half the women featured here are "female firsts," such as GM's Barra, the most world's most powerful businesswoman and Fed Chair Janet Yellen, the top global state banker. Drew Gilpin Faust is the first female president of Harvard, Folorunsho Alakija is the first self-made African billionaire and Sara Blakely was the first female self-made billionaire to sign The Giving Pledge, Bill Gates and Warren Buffett's bid to encourage the world's richest to give at least half their wealth to charity. And then there's Hillary Clinton. Her CV is chock full of firsts: the only first lady to become a U.S. Senator turned Secretary of State turned two-time presidential candidate. As a 2016 candidate, bets were on that she may be the first woman elected to the Oval Office, although that was not how it turned out in the end.

Women in tech: Technology takes a fourth turn as a category on the Power Women list. Out of eighteen in total, seven tech women made the Top 25 this year, including Sandberg, YouTube's CEO Susan Wojcicki, IBM's Ginni Rometty, HP's Meg Whitman and Yahoo CEO Marissa Mayer.

The rising tide of female entrepreneurs: A remarkable number of women are founders or owners of their own enterprises, not a few of whose eponymous companies are synonymous with high fashion. Consider Miuccia Prada, Tory Burch and Diane von Furstenberg. Other self-made self-starters include Winfrey, Alibaba's co-founder Lucy Peng, billionaire founder-CEO Elizabeth Holmes, Chinese real estate tycoon Zhang Xin and Kiran Mazumdar-Shaw, India's first biotech entrepreneur.

Geographic diversity: More than half of the women (59) on the list are American, including immigrants such as von Furstenberg (Belgium), Ambassador Samantha Power (Ireland), Weili

Dai (China), Donna Langley (UK) and Padmasree Warrior (India). Asia-Pacific citizens make the second strongest showing at eighteen. Latin America and the Middle East have four regionals on the list and there are twelve Europeans and three Africans with a slot.

STEM degrees' payoff: On this year's list, along with the expected M.B.A.s and law degrees, there is a healthy dose of women who earned degrees in science, technology, engineering and math. Five are medical doctors, including Polish President Kopacz, Chilean President Michelle Bachelet and Margaret Chan of the World Health Organization. More unexpected STEM degree-holders include Merkel (PhD in chemistry), Dupont CEO Ellen Kullman (mechanical engineering), Sheikh Lubna Al Qasimi (computer science) and Judith Faulkner (mathematics).

The new celebrity role models: Sure, they're famous, but they deserve special attention outside their day jobs. Oprah founded both Harpo Productions and The Oprah Winfrey Leadership Academy for Girls in South Africa. Joining the efforts of the U.N. are Angelina Jolie, Shakira and Yao Chen, the Refugee Agency's Goodwill Ambassador in China. Taylor Swift donated five figures to the New York City Department of Education from sales of "Welcome to New York" and promises to continue to give if the song sells. Entertainers making a mint as entrepreneurs include Beyoncé and Sofia Vergara.

Healing, feeding and educating the world: If they're not topping corporations or state, the women on our list are heads of major non-profit and intergovernmental organisations and they wield huge budgets and impact millions, from Gates, Laurene Powell Jobs and Bloomberg's Patricia Harris to World Food Programme Executive Director Ertharin Cousin and Harvard's Faust.

UNIT 32

IS IT THE RIGHT TIME TO BE A WOMAN?

There has been a considerable amount of media attention in the UK in 2015 around this subject and I most certainly do not agree with this statement. I would explore the world in why I challenge this statement.

EXAMPLE ONE – INDIA – SEPTEMBER 2015

- Meenakshi Kumari, 23, was sentenced for rape alongside 15-year-old sister
- Feared un-elected council of upper-caste men ordered savage punishment
- Brother ran away with married woman with whom he had two-year affair
- Family has appealed to India's Supreme Court and Prime Minister for help

EXAMPLE TWO – IRAQ – 2015

The Yazidi religious minority community in Iraq says 3,500 of its women and girls are still being held by the so-called Islamic State (IS), many being used as sex slaves. A few have managed to escape and tell their harrowing stories.

EXAMPLE 3 – RAPE CULTURE

Rape – We have the right to say NO! In the UK, each year 85,000 women are raped or suffer serious sexual assault. Only 1,070 rapists are convicted. Rape Culture filled the 70's – did we not protect against violence against women? In the USA Bill Crosby admitted to drugging women for sex. So, this TV star can boast about it.

RAPE CULTURE – is the concern of young girls going to their GP's with horrific internal injuries because their boyfriends watched pornos and pressurised them into anal sex? Though this is something that women in certain Muslim communities can identify with, as even in their marriages they are vehicles to yield children and to provide pleasure, their men would prefer anal sex – is that for economic reasons or that they prefer anal sex?

We need to protect and warn our daughters against the possibility of rape and explain to our sons the importance of consent. This rape culture is very much alive and thriving.

When I was raped in Italy in the grounds of a Thompson hotel in Sorrento, I was not protected because the rapist was not a member of staff. Thompson would not take any responsibility for this crime, even with all the details the rapists knew about the hotel. A date rape drug was put in my drink in a bar near the hotel and the rapists followed me back to my hotel, only five minutes away. They had done it before, they knew the location and layout of the hotel—knew that the carpark would be open, that I had to pass it to access the hotel and that after 11 p.m. the hotel main door would be closed. They also knew that I had to ring for attention and that this would take time. They used this knowledge to attack me from behind, knock me unconscious with a claw hammer and drag me to the car park adjacent. And here is some more disturbing news: The accomplice in this heinous crime was a woman, a lover of the rapist. Her bite marks were found around my private parts.

It is incredible that someone who I used to greatly admire, the Rock Chick of the 70's, Chrissie Hynde, had to apologise on UK daytime TV for asking the audience, "Is rape a woman's fault?" So, if you wear a short skirt, are you asking for it? Responsibility for rape will always lie with the perpetrator—always. Chrissie, shame on you; and you stated that you were raped by Hells Angels?

There are horrific stories coming out of universities in the UK, about the culture of using rape as a dare or as an entrance to a certain group. On one hand, we were told how bright we were and how the future was ours to be anything we wanted; and then, on the other hand, we would be joking with our girlfriends about a date that went wrong – we were drunk – cannot remember and it happened. But it was rape! In 2015 one in three women on university campuses across the UK were sexually assaulted. When we are young, we shrug it off as if it is our fault—nothing to moan about because, after all, I was drunk! They are "Blurred Lines," as in the song, and that is why I shake with fear when I hear that most popular tune—it was playing that night in the bar when I had my drink spiked.

Through my therapy at present, I must undergo this nightmare every week to be free. It is so painful and it has made me physically ill for the past four weeks, with several chest infections. But it must be done, to heal and to take away the power of the rapists over your life.

I wanted to leave you with this Woman Warrior Violette Szabo, who quoted a poem by Leo Marks, "The Life That I Have." Violette was a Woman Warrior in the Second World War, a British Spy who was awarded the George Cross; only four other females have been given the George Cross. The film *Carve Her Name with Pride* was made about her, and her bravery behind enemy lines will be immortalised in my memory and that of others forever.

I have been trying to be a "Woman Warrior," I feel, since I was at nursery school, aged two, and in defiance did not play with the Wendy house with dolls, but plonked myself in the sand pit with the boys to build castles. These days I am building my business and those of others and in particular take great pride in supporting other Women Warriors. If you wish to contact me about any support, do not hesitate to contact me at karen@gateway2enterprise.co.uk. I wish you a loving, fulfilled, happy life. It is our duty to take care of other women as they need us.

In 2016 I went through a Divorce that I did not want I still love my ex-husband but I knew it was coming and we will remain always great friends. He has always been supportive of me. Wishing love and happiness with his new wife Faten.

I had to completely restructure my business to survive lost some people along the way some that I was keen to see the back of and some who I will miss. Gained some new great people, though.

I am on a new journey of DISCOVERY to find me again – to learn – live and share and be that 'Woman Warrior' to lift others!

I would like to leave you with a quote ' **First they ignore you**, then they laugh at you, then they fight you, then you win." - Mahatma **Gandhi. This always lifts me up to fight another day as a 'Woman Warrior'.**

UNIT 33

BERLIN KEYNOTE SPEAKER/COMPERE GLOBAL WOMEN'S LEADERSHIP CONFERENCE 2016 NOV

In November 2016 I had the honour and privilege to be the Key Note Speaker and Compere for the Global Women's Leadership Conference in Berlin. I was so flattered and though was busy with my own work running two companies I felt it was my duty to support other women. My Key Note was Realities for Financial Security for women – whether in business – in the home or at work. I had to open the Conference after my colleague Sarah Hopwood Speaker and BBC Presenter had given me such a welcoming introduction. Opening a Conference is a tough job but with women only well that is a lot tougher. I had to deliver a 2-hour workshop and I was happy with my Presentation and it was received well and the follow up from the group of women was as I predicted 25% of 50 women. With a male lead conference I do receive and expect 99% and that is because men are easier to please and will only take in the facts of the Presentation of what they learnt whereas women way up other women on their looks weight accent dress code age and more. Women are a lot harder on other women. In 2016 I only delivered two women lead conferences and I do tend to limit my time spent in this arena. My hope for the future is that women could learn to love themselves and other women to support them on their journey. Stop seeing women as competition to you as a woman but as an enable to achieve your goals. Most women are sexual predators and that I feel is because of choosing a mate to conceive and multiply so it is their biological clock hormones that make us so unkind to other women. I was brought up in a family where my grandmother, mother and sister do not embrace and love other women. I feel that because I am lead more by my male Y chromosome. This is called 'QUEEN BEE' syndrome and even dating back to the 1970's research was being undertaken As Sheryl Sandberg and Adam Grant point out in their essay in *The New York Times* on the myth of the catty woman, this belief rests on the erroneous idea that there is something inherent to the female sex that causes women to undermine each other on the job all the time.

There is the other syndrome of the 'RIGHTEOUS WOMAN' this is the mantle that I have always taken why would I not support other women after all it is our duty. The Righteous Woman is an ideal, a belief that women have a distinct moral obligation to have one another's backs. This kind of sentiment is best typified by Madeleine Albright's now famous quote, "There is a special place in hell for women who don't help each other!" The basic idea is that since all women experience sexism, they should be more attuned to the gendered barriers that other women face. In turn, this heightened awareness should lead women to foster alliances and actively support one another. If women don't help each other, this is an even worse form of betrayal than those committed by men. And hence, the special place in hell reserved for those women.

I worked hard with my colleague Sarah to make the Conference knowledgeable but fun and when Sarah and I appraised the Conference we felt that as we worked as a great team and it was teamwork it was achieved. Thank you to the HALCON Group for these Conferences to enable other women who are so talented to share our knowledge, skills and our own personal journey. I also say to myself, 'that is I reach just one person in a group and make a difference then I have done my job' And at this Conference it as Alex Micu who have up her corporate job in Recruitment in Europe to start her own business Talentcentre and within 2 years she has 260 clients. I know that in 2017 I will be mentoring Alex to bring her business model to the UK.

Thank you a lot.

It is very important for me to have your support. Alex sent me this little message. So I was of some use at the Conference.

HELP US TO RAISE FUNDS FOR SAMANTHA AND HER CHILDREN

Sam is a brave Woman Warrior who needs to raise £130k for a life-saving brain operation in the USA. Sam has her own business to support her two children and I would like you to donate through her Crowdfunding campaign to support her journey of being an independent Mum and a true Woman Warrior.

Sam has less than four months to raise funds for the neurosurgery and she is deteriorating at a fast rate. We need to raise funds before Sam is too ill to fly abroad for the surgery to the USA.

Here is the link to the Crowdfunding Campaign; giving what you can is truly appreciated

https://www.youcaring.com/samanthasmith-788861

Granada Reports (ITV North West) have done a TV report on the 6 o'clock news which is available via this link

http://www.itv.com/news/granada/2017-04-14/crushed-by-her-own-skull-the-single-mum-from-rochdale-hoping-for-life-saving-treatment/

and the Huffington Post UK did a report here

http://www.huffingtonpost.co.uk/entry/samantha-smith-plea-for-life-saving-surgery-abroad-for-ehlers-danlos-syndrome_uk_58f87c00e4b0cb086d7e3237

Trinity Mirror have asked to cover the stories and the Manchester Evening News are following her progress and fundraising events.

Join Sam on Facebook, let us support her journey www.facebook.com/savingsamantha

I will be donating myself so TOGETHER we can 'make a difference' save Sam's life and allow her to continue being a loving, caring Mum of two.

Thank you in advance for your support,

Karen

CPSIA information can be obtained
at www.ICGtesting.com
Printed in the USA
LVOW10s1747060418
572582LV00011B/883/P

9 781628 654967